THE POETRY OF POSTMODERNITY

Also by Dennis Brown

INTERTEXTUAL DYNAMICS WITHIN THE LITERARY
CROWD – JOYCE, LEWIS, POUND AND ELIOT:
The Men of 1914

MS MOFFAT
(*under the pseudonym Ned Brown*)

THE MODERNIST SELF IN TWENTIETH-CENTURY
ENGLISH LITERATURE:
A Study in Self-Fragmentation

The Poetry of Postmodernity

Anglo/American Encodings

Dennis Brown
Professor
Department of English
University of Hertfordshire

First published in Great Britain 1994 by
THE MACMILLAN PRESS LTD
Houndmills, Basingstoke, Hampshire RG21 2XS
and London
Companies and representatives
throughout the world

A catalogue record for this book is available
from the British Library.

ISBN 0–333–60473–3

Printed and bound in Great Britain by
Biddles Ltd, Guildford and King's Lynn

First published in the United States of America 1994 by
Scholarly and Reference Division,
ST. MARTIN'S PRESS, INC.,
175 Fifth Avenue,
New York, N.Y. 10010

ISBN 0–312–12093–1

Library of Congress Cataloging-in-Publication Data
Brown, Dennis, 1940–
The poetry of postmodernity : Anglo/American encodings / Dennis Brown.
p.   cm.
Includes index.
ISBN 0–312–12093–1
1. English poetry—20th century—History and criticism.
2. American poetry—20th century—History and criticism.
3. Modernism (Literature)—Great Britain.   4. Modernism
(Literature)—United States.   I. Title.
PR478.M6B73   1994
821′.9109—dc20   93–48922
                                                                      CIP

8   7   6   5   4   3   2
03   02   01   00   99   98   97

In memory of

Elsie Worvill (1916–91)
George Macbeth (1932–92), poet
Nola Clendinning Pechey (1943–93), artist

In the electric age we wear all mankind as our skin
Marshall McLuhan

Contents

Preface

This book was written between the winter of 1991–2 and the spring of 1993: the specific time frame seems important in terms of the ongoing postmodernism debate – as we race towards the double millennium. Such a declaration inevitably owns to its temporal partiality and implies a fairly imminent sell-by date. In Wyndham Lewis's description, we are all "time snobs" now: both the pace of global developments and the instantaneity of communications constantly outflank any attempt to make a fixed map of the contemporary scene. This is, in fact, what makes the discussion of 'postmodernity' continuous, contingent, confusing – and exciting. In such a situation it seems necessary to date a particular stage of one's thinking: so I shall 'sign' this as of Easter 1993.

I should like here to thank Peter Widdowson for cannily pointing me, nearly three years ago, towards the direction I was going in – without my then knowing it. Thanks, too, to the East London (and FAB) 'Psychoanalysis and the Public Sphere' conferences where two of the chapters below were tried out and whose discussions have helped form my own sense of the nature of postmodernity. Also thanks to the encouragement or advice of Phil Ballard, Eibhlin Evans, Paul Gatland, Patrick Grant, Graham Holderness, Sarah Hutton, Sharon Monteith, Graham Pechey, Jean Radford, Eric Trudgill and George Wotton, and to Zygmunt Bauman whose book *Intimations of Postmodernity* came out at a crucial stage of my own project and who responded, in detail, to some material I sent him – "in the spirit of dialogue".

The writing of this book has coincided with the welcome transformation of my teaching base from Hatfield Polytechnic to the University of Hertfordshire. With its roots in a gift of land by A. S. Butler of De Havilland, our institution has itself played a role in the construction of postmodern realities – most particularly in aero-engineering, information science, psychology and pharmacological biochemistry: it has been a privilege to serve on research committees with representatives of such disciplines. The work below originated in a research project registered with our old Research and Consultancy Committee.

My conviction in the book is that certain Anglo/American poets understood the direction in which contemporary culture was going long before "postmodernity" was theorised. One of the book's dedicatees, George Macbeth – whose recent death came as a personal shock – helped foster their work during his years at the BBC. I believe that poetry can retain its prophetic function and I hope what I have written will encourage students to keep reading it – both yesterday's and tomorrow's as well as today's.

Lastly, I must particularly thank my wife, Sam, whose "formatting" has cleaned up my "keyboarding" on that amazing postmodern phenomenon, the word-processor. Deepest thanks, too (and again), for her unfailing moral support:

> Let the urge of mere ambition
> Seek success in what we do,
> Find direction where we go:
> In each other know completion.

DENNIS BROWN

1

Introduction

I have called this book *The Poetry of Postmodernity*. The situational term "postmodernity" signals a residual suspicion of the word "postmodernism" – and of its necessary relevance to poetry of the recent era. Nevertheless, I accept that the concept of the postmodern is now well established and the poetry I shall discuss has been largely chosen for the way it negotiates issues said to be characteristic of the postmodern situation and its aesthetic. Much of the point of the book (what some critics might call its "intervention") is that little has been written about poetry itself in a postmodern context. Much has been written about a new cultural phenomenon (variously dated in the period since the Second World War).[1] Much has also now been published concerning post-modernist architecture, film, fiction, video, performance and even music.[2] There is a frequently cited text entitled *A Poetics of Postmodernism*[3] which scarcely alludes to actual poetry, poems or poets at all. Indeed, most recent literary uses of the concept have applied it, almost exclusively, to novelistic output over the last few years. Yet if we really inhabit a "condition"[4] of postmodernity, it must surely, somehow, have manifested itself in British and American poetry too. "Artists are the antennae of the race" Ezra Pound asserted, thinking primarily of poetry: my book attempts to test that aphorism as it applies to selected samples of poetry written in the era termed postmodern.

The construction of postmodernism is a relatively recent theo-retical accomplishment – a matter of, say, some twenty years at the most. The term had been tentatively used earlier and the sense of a general cultural phenomenon began to crystallise in the mid-1970s.[5] However, the ongoing ferment of debate, in Britain at least, stems largely from the translation of Jean-François Lyotard's book *The Postmodern Condition* and the flood of commentary that came in its wake. The declared aim of this cogent pamphlet was to report on the state of "knowledge" and, indeed, there is much in it about computers, information theory, cybernetics and the problem of legitimising scientific theories and practices. Yet, in addition, the book inevitably raised questions about international finance, intellectual property and the control of knowledge; it also alluded to *avant-garde* practices in the arts and, in general, evoked the spectre of an unprecedented international revolution affecting everything from video games to projective scenarios of nuclear war. In the later, somewhat manic-depressive, writings of Jean Baudrillard[6] such a vision became fanned to whiteheat and easily infiltrated an Anglo-Saxon critical culture already dazzled into Gallicism by the deconstruction of Jacques Derrida and others. Marxist critics such as Fredric Jameson[7] and Terry Eagleton[8] became alerted and recognised, at a blink, the chimeric deceptions and mystifications of the final stand of late, Late Capitalism. Thereafter, just about everyone got in on the act: postmodernism was linked to poststructuralism, allied to feminism[9] and theorised in relation to postcolonialism. A great new ISM was born: an ISM, it seemed, which could never become a WASM. Books poured from the academic presses – indeed no text on contemporary culture which omitted the buzz-word from its title was likely to get a reader's report, never mind publication.

However, much that has been mooted under the slogan of post-modernism had been said, more pithily, in the sixties by Marshall McLuhan. With the rare exception of Baudrillard,[10] the name and ideas of McLuhan have been scandalously absent from the whole debate. Possibly French intellectuals like Lyotard were too over-whelmed by "les événements" of 1968 (that over-glorified farce) to have been reading the work of a practitioner of Canadian English. But the English-speaking world (despite Jonathan Miller's[11] wanton and misleading attack on McLuhan in the "Modern Masters" series) ought to have arrived at postmodernism already. It was the "electric age" and in *The Gutenberg Galaxy* and *Understanding Media*[12] McLuhan had epigrammatically announced some of its main features and showed how it was in the process of decon-structing textual rationality long before Derrida became a mantra-word in the literary academy.

Of course, McLuhan had help – in the form of a World War Two friendship with the exiled Wyndham Lewis[13] who in *BLAST* (1914) had launched something in England normally known as modernism. McLuhan's journal was called *COUNTERBLAST* (his book by this name was published in Britain in 1970) and helped develop Lewis's ideas and typographical strategies. In which regard, it is interesting that Fredric Jameson, one of the more prolific commentators on the postmodern in English, has also written a notable book on Lewis[14] – though his monumental tome *Postmodernism* – part-based on Lewis's *The Art of Being Ruled* and *Time and Western Man*? – does not even mention Lewis in the index.

The case for seeing Lewis as an originator of the postmodern argument is disputatious – and I have touched on it elsewhere. Here I should like, briefly, to press the merits of McLuhan's largely neglected contribution. For in stressing the unique peculiarities of the "electric age" he pointed to fundamental issues which now dominate discussions of postmodernity – however much one may wish to distance oneself from his "dot" theory of television or his millenarian euphoria. Put in the crudest terms, McLuhan distinguished between tribal orality, manuscript culture, the "Gutenberg Galaxy" (meaning print culture as the mechanisation of writing) and the "electric age". The first three have received sustained research and commentary over many years – without, I feel, radically undermining McLuhan's findings, which were themselves based on established scholarship. His real breakthrough consisted of his diagnosis that the "electric age" constituted something wholly unprecedented – the coming of the new media put all in doubt.

In particular, McLuhan insisted that television symbolised a new era of global intercommunication which could not merely be subsumed within metanarratives about the progress of Western knowledge, the distribution of power "centres" or the dominance of some economic "base". Television, he thought, altered the very basis of conceptual understanding itself, through its instantaneous plenitude of information and its iconic mode of transmission and reception and that rendered theoretical metanarrative obsolete. In this, I believe, he was largely right – as well as ahead of the game. An informational paradigm shift had occurred which he identified. McLuhan expounded postmodernity in all but name and he also suggested many "consequences" which are now generally labelled postmodernist.

The very term "postmodernism" invokes the prior concept of modernism – however we manipulate the prefix. But in the current debate postmodernism is frequently set in relation to "modernity" rather than modernism. In Britain, for many years, the term "modernism" denoted the artistic and cultural movement which in literature abolished textual continuity (Joyce and Eliot – both associated with *BLAST*), in music abolished harmony (Stravinsky and Schoenberg) and in painting, abolished perspective (Picasso, Kandinsky, Klee *et al.*). However, a cultural commentator like Jürgen Habermas[15] uses "modernity" in a wholly different way. For him, "modernity" denotes the rational, emancipatory programme from the Enlightenment onwards (a programme which Eliot and Lewis in many ways opposed). Modernity is a very different concept from modernism. Texts like *The Waste Land* and Ezra Pound's *Cantos* or *Finnegans Wake* are neither "rational", evidently emancipatory (in the political sense), nor programmatic (beyond aesthetic principles). They work to *re*mythologise the *de*mythologisation discourse of the Enlightenment and are modernist precisely by subverting the whole Western "Will to Truth".[16] One ingenious way out of this confusion has been suggested in a recent book by Thomas Docherty[17] which invites us to see *The Waste Land* (and by extension, I take it, other such texts) as, in fact, *post*-modernist. One sees what he is getting at, but the preference of this book will be to call the art of late "modernity" modernism and the Enlightenment project the Enlightenment project.

The example of architecture in this century has also enormously complicated the issue – the more so when a literary critic like Linda Hutcheon takes architectural *post*modernism as her bench-mark.[18] In the early years of the century, architecture and literature were alike in one important respect: both were resolved to "MAKE IT NEW". For architects, this meant pure innovation and they had brand new materials to use; for writers, it meant to *re*new, as well as to originate and they had to adapt familiar materials of form and language. Eliot's crucial essay "Tradition and the Individual Talent" modified the stance of *BLAST* and anticipated the method of *Ulysses*, *The Waste Land* and the *Cantos*. Literary newness was to be set in uneasy relationship to the past: in practice, through allusion, quotation, structural paralleling, parody and pastiche – the characteristics most often cited with respect to *post*modern architecture. Modernist architecture was totalitarian, functionalist and structuralist, while modernist "high" literature was collagistic, aestheticist and "poststructuralist": there could scarcely be a greater contrast. For this reason, the transition between modernist and postmodern literature is quite continuous, subtle and recapitulatory, whereas in architecture there is a near total difference. Briefly, if we wish to interrogate the nature of poetic production within postmodernism, with any real insight, it is better to ignore the case of architecture altogether.

Literary modernism, seen overall, is a far more complex, even paradoxical, matter than is commonly acknowledged. Early modernists (or perhaps precursors) such as Henry James, Joseph Conrad and Ford Madox Hueffer had managed to combine stylistic experimentation with relatively conventional moral standards. Within the "Men of 1914"[19] – Joyce, Lewis, Pound and Eliot – there were differences of emphasis which could develop into intellectual and artistic battles – Lewis damning *Ulysses* as "passéist,[20] for instance or Pound declaring of *Finnegans Wake* "nothing short of divine vision or a new cure for the clapp (*sic*) can possibly be worth all the circumambient peripherization."[21] Virginia Woolf was a friend of Eliot but Lewis attacked her for "plagiarism"[22] and her more overtly modernist texts – *Mrs Dalloway, To the Lighthouse* and *The Waves* – manifest none of the preoccupation with archaic mythology which characterises the work of Joyce, Pound and Eliot.

However, D. H. Lawrence *was* interested in primitive rites and ancient symbolism, yet his more conventional narrative strategies make many critics doubt how far he was modernist at all. Lewis's early style was spectacularly Vorticist (and he learnt much from Futurism) but, again, his rigidly external satiric grotesquerie set him at odds with the fluxive, interior fluidity of Imagism or the stream-of-consciousness method. Further, May Sinclair, Dorothy Richardson, Rebecca West and Katherine Mansfield, among other women, were clearly involved in the overall modernist movement, yet what they achieved was very different from *Ulysses* or *The Waste Land*, the prototypical modernist texts. In short, literary modernism did not achieve any monolithic consensus like that of the architectural Functionalists, rather it offered a rich portfolio of expressive possibilities to its postmodern heirs.

The whole inheritance becomes even more complicated if American modernism and varieties of neomodernism are put in the balance. Wallace Stevens has had a clear influence on the work of John Ashbery (arguably the clearest case of a "postmodernist" poet), but Stevens' poetry is quite different from that of Pound, Eliot or HD. Similarly, William Carlos Williams, whose work has affinities with Imagism, was appalled when first confronted with the phenomenon of *The Waste Land*.[23] William Faulkner may have learnt from Joyce's technique, yet he is as much a regionalist in the manner of Thomas Hardy, while John Dos Passos' *USA* exploited a neomodernist "historiographic metafiction" which Jameson finds unique in

E. L. Doctorow's *Ragtime* and Hutcheon makes the leading principle of the postmodern aesthetic.

On this side of the Atlantic, David Jones' *In Parenthesis* represents a neomodernist version of trench realism while his *Anathemata*[24] spectacularly extends the modernist tradition into the 1950s – an achievement which Basil Bunting's *Briggflatts*[25] continued into the mid-sixties. Samuel Beckett, as much a disciple of Joyce and Lewis[26] as Jones was of Eliot or Bunting of Pound, seems more neomodernist than postmodern (though his work has been claimed for postmodernism) and his writing continued on almost into the nineties. And how should we place the fiction of B. S. Johnson or the poetry of George MacBeth – neomodernist or early post-modernist? ... The issues are complex, the labels arbitrary and the arguments potentially endless. With architecture, it is otherwise – as, also, with television, hi-fi or video, if only for reasons of technological advance. Poetry is different and distinctive; the poetry of postmodernity does not assert a clear rift with modernism nor even proclaim a wholly unparalleled "condition". Rather, it maintains a dialogue with poetic modernism and neomodernism to help interrogate just what the cultural situation *is*.

In the Western world, the sixties represented the cultural moment when the unique realities of the "electric age" were becoming apparent. If the "radio" babble of *The Waste Land* and *Finnegans Wake* had acted as a kind of early-warning device, the actualities of commercialised electronics now seeped throughout a world whose cultural mind-set was still structured by the previous textual hegemony. But television, new sound systems and satellite communications were increasingly undermining that hegemony. Furthermore, for anyone in or near a university, the computer represented a portentous new intellectual idol, shortly to be transformed into the Trojan Horse of the information revolution in offices, schools and eventually homes. While French intellectuals were still tinkering with base-superstructure models of the social realm, the new realities were hardware and software, un-"based" satellite architectonics and the seamless web of electronic information where every margin was itself a centre. McLuhan, for all his excesses, knew what was going on, Sartre and Althusser, for all their brilliance, did not. Nor, indeed, did the editors of *The New Left Review* as they fell under the spell of Paris. McLuhan could be dismissed as a Catholic "organicist" as Lewis had been firmly labelled a "Fascist". So it was that the postmodern condition remained to be constituted by a French academic at the end of the seventies. By then the "electric age" had found its *philosophe*: he wrote – and all the intellectuals cried "Amen".

The seventies, as a whole, helped prepare the way for this belated recognition of the "electric age" and its socio-cultural and intellectual implications. There seem to have been several factors involved. In France, the *nouveau roman* had helped to provide a bridge between modernism and postmodernism (at a time when England reverted to neoGeorgianism in verse and suburban realism in prose). This created a degree of mutuality between creative writers and progressive thinkers which fed into the poststructuralism of such as Jacques Derrida, Michel Foucault and later Roland Barthes, with Lyotard and Baudrillard, most particularly, in a position to deconstruct the Marxian narratives which had so long entranced the Left Bank.

In addition, the rise of American, British and French feminism was beginning to dissolve those Patriarchal/Rationalist/Textualist certainties which had kept the Enlightenment project on its iron tracks, despite the major sabotage of modernist aesthetics. Most particularly, the new writing practices of such as Julia Kristeva, Luce Irigaray and Hélène Cixous (together with Mary Daley in the United States) helped subvert the "Gutenberg" mentality which had hitherto largely withstood both modernist *écriture féminine* and the realities of the "electric age". Textual language as a web, as intuitive fluidity and as psychic and bodily expression, rather than as mere linear-logical machine, began to be extended from the aesthetic experimentation of such as Richardson, Joyce and Woolf into socio-critical commentary itself. Further, new advances in video technology, the dissemination of computerisation and the additional globalisation of finance enforced, even more, the consequences of electronic takeover. Finally, the imaginative pioneering of North and South American writers like Kurt Vonnegut, Jorge Luis Borges, Gabriel Garcia Marquez, Thomas Pynchon or John Hawkes (itself in touch with earlier international modernism) began to bear fruit in such British writers as Angela Carter, D. M. Thomas and Salman Rushdie. By the early eighties, with influential plays like Tom Stoppard's *Jumpers* and *Travesties* already behind it, a postmodern fiction was well into stride even on the island fortress of empiricism.

The eighties was the grand decade of the postmodern. This was as much in terms of critical theory as artistic production. Once

named, the "electric age" was almost everywhere acknowledged –
even by some historians. A strange variant of Anselm's "ontological"
proof began to be put about: it insinuated that postmodernism
existed because its systemic presence had been postulated and
everyone was talking about it.[27] In fact, the term itself was
inextricably implicated in the phenomenon it set out to describe: it
became highly fashionable, increasingly international and continuously fuelled by the advertising gimmicks of Late Capitalism,
in the form of book titles, journalism, television coverage and the
creation of degree courses which invoked it. By the summer of 1990
the *Times Higher Education Supplement* (shortly to be postmodernised as *The Higher*) was prompted to publish four con-
secutive leaders on "The Postmodern Challenge".[28] The "electric
age" had come into its own as postmodernism, while the old
geopolitical certainties began to fall apart on twenty-four hour
cable and satellite television. The eve of the 1991 Gulf War
provided a striking vignette of the postmodern cultural implosion
when CNN hypnotically broadcast world-wide images of a
handwritten Iraqi note being hustled past Picasso's "Guernica" in
the foyer of the United Nations building. To play off Beckett's
Endgame: whatever it was called, something was "taking its
course".

However, if one agrees to call this something "postmodernism",
has it necessarily produced its own aesthetic? Many critics insist that
it has and have attempted to describe it. Yet it is striking that most of
the characteristics claimed as typical of postmodern art were already
inherent in modernist texts. Thus, despite Brian McHale's subtle
argument in *Postmodernist Fiction*,[29] there is both epistemological *and*
ontological crisis in texts like *The Waste Land, Finnegans Wake* or the
Pisan *Cantos*. Such texts are also rich in parody and pastiche –
features which Linda Hutcheon ascribes specifically to postmodern
fictions. It was modernist literature, not postmodern architecture,
which pioneered "quotational" reference to past historical styles and,
despite the élitist *address* of *Ulysses* and *The Waste Land*, they made
considerable use of populist material – pub-talk, popular song,
novelette scenarios, advertising slogans or nursery rhyme – thus
eroding the distinction between highbrow and lowbrow. Even the
exploitation of fantasy *zones*[30] was initiated in Lewis's *The Childermass*
and Joyce's *Wake*.

The argument applies to almost all the specified qualities of
postmodern art. Generic instability, "theatrical" fictionality, sur-

face interplay, anamnesis, eschatological anxiety or the relativ-isation of language games – all these can be evidenced in modernist texts. This seems to suggest that literary modernism and postmodernism are more nearly synonyms than antonyms. Postmodern aesthetics might simply be regarded as an adaptation of features tried out within modernism to represent a more speci-fically "electric" era. From a "high" aesthetic standpoint, it might even be suggested that the postmodern aesthetic, in so far as it exists, is modernism pursued through more facile means.

A cultural "condition" is one thing, the practice and theory of art another: it would be naïve "reflectionism" to expect any necessarily direct relation between the two. In fact, it is clear that much creative production continues much as before, whatever the experience of modernity or postmodernity. For every Joyce there are many Bennetts or Buchans, for every Pound many Masefields or Brookes. This is just as much the case in writing since the Second World War – even in the postmodernist eighties. There is nothing very postmodern about the writings of, for example, Kingsley Amis, Frederick Forsyth, Seamus Heaney, John le Carré or Tom Sharpe. And this is not just the reality in writing: for every *Blade Runner* there are dozens of *Rocky* or *Police Academy* movies, for every *Twin Peaks* there are dozens of television soap operas, for every David Bowie there are hundreds of schlock pop lyricists. Even if one could define the postmodern condition quite exactly, there is no guar-antee that even "serious" artists would agree on a uniform aesthetic to express it. Rather, we should expect what will be evidenced below – a range of artistic techniques and standpoints deployed to interrogate and give voice to our experience of the postmodern.

However, the method of procedure here will not be merely eclectic. I have chosen to focus on those poets who not only alert us to unique features of the postmodern world but also write in aware dialogue with the artists of literary modernism. The Movement poets, for instance, did not: they sought to return to Georgian or even Augustan conventions,[31] away from both modernist experimentation and the implications of the "electric age". Philip Larkin summed up what he rejected in the names Picasso, Pound and Charlie Parker; Kingsley Amis added, at least, Dylan Thomas and Stravinsky. Such attitudes spring from some nostalgic premodernism rather than any relevant postmodernism and need not concern this book. The poets considered below tended to recognise the modernist writers as prophets rather than charlatans:

that, one might suggest, is an aspect of their postmodern credentials.

The "cultural production" of poetry in America and Britain since the Second World War requires a separate book devoted entirely to the subject. Yet some realities should briefly be acknowledged here. Considered sociologically, printed poetry has been an almost negligible epiphenomenon within recent "Fordism" and "post-Fordism" – tenuously supported in terms of paltry grants, university manuscript collection and the sale of books to students in particular. The establishment of a poetic reputation has often been a lengthy and uncertain process – of the poets considered below, neither Allen Ginsberg not Geoffrey Hill, in particular, have yet achieved the recognition I think they deserve. In theirs, as in other cases, "little presses" have played a vital role in initial publication – providing the possibility of critical attention and eventual consideration by the large publishing houses. In the case of Auden, Hughes and Plath, in particular, Faber and Faber (presided over by the discriminatory spirit of T. S Eliot) has constituted the vital launching pad. Both Berryman and Ashbery were able to use the network of American literary periodicals as a springboard for book publication, while Thomas's early career was enabled (in terms of presses) through the Welsh connection, until the "Penguin Modern Poets" series helped him attain a wider audience.

All the poets considered below have been lucky – their work has been noticed. They represent the shining tips of an iceberg of recent poetic expression in English. In practice, the cultural production of printed poetry remains a hit-and-miss affair – facilitated through the efforts of dedicated weirdos, the judgments of publishing-house editors and the uncertain magnanimity of reviewers in minority newspapers. If the work of a poet prospers, it eventually attains mainstream publication (in small print-runs), becomes co-opted onto academic syllabuses and receives the, largely retrospective, attention of university critics (such as myself). The cultural production of contemporary poetry is very much a tale of survival and development against the odds. However, from my standpoint in the arena of reception, it cannot be the process of "production" but the nature of the poetic product which really matters.

It must be pointed out that the writers chosen below are essentially print-text poets. It seems important to acknowledge this, since there is a powerful argument to be made that the characteristic poetry of postmodernity consists, in fact, of the lyrics of such as Bob

Dylan, John Lennon, Jim Morrison, David Bowie, Van Morrison or Elvis Costello. In some respects I accept this view: it seems to me, for instance, that the lyrics of John Lennon are both more representative and more international than, say, the poems of Thom Gunn or Margaret Atwood. Whereas Ezra Pound used to lament a divorce between textual lyric and heard music since the seventeenth century, the new electronic troubadours have importantly re-established the old consonance. But the "electric age" lyric or "ballad" is not quite the same as its older oral equivalent – as textuality is even more to be distinguished from "orality".[32] The pop lyric needs to be assessed in terms of the combined word-sound blend once it has left the sound studio, not in terms of textual "sense" – and, indeed, conventional literary criticism has never done very well in discussing words chosen for music, whether "Loude sing cuckou!" or "Ding-dong, bell" or "The times they are a-changin'".

This is a work of criticism rather than a cultural studies analysis and I have focused on poets who work within print-text constraints to explore and express postmodern realities. My choice of poets is inevitably restricted: my enthusiasm for aspects of the eight chosen poets' contribution will be evident, but my aim is less to canonise than to diagnose. I am somewhat embarrassed by the inclusion of only one woman poet; however, it seems to me that the work of such poets as, say, HD, Adrienne Rich, Maya Angelou or Anne Stevenson is diagnostic of something beyond the condition of the postmodern, as normally described. It would be good to have a book called, perhaps, *The Poetry of Postmodern Feminism* – but a woman should (surely) have written it.

My book, then, has a somewhat partial aim – to study certain selected poets for what they can tell us about the postmodern world. However, I do not regard this as a marginal task. After all, the key theorisations of the postmodern are themselves written in print-text words (they are not image collages or *musique concrète* or computer codes). They seek to comprehend the "electric age" in essentially "Gutenberg" terms, whether written on a word-processor or not. Jean-François Lyotard makes much of language games (but in a metadiscourse akin to the return of narrative). Marshall McLuhan made much of media "probes" (in a specially chosen academic "ad-speak" of aphorism, anecdote, adage, exemplum and pun). Beyond these two, most of the commentaries conform to the conventions of the academic monograph (as this book must) –

sometimes in a polysyllabic theory-jargon worthy only of Pseuds' Corner.

Textual poetry has traditionally occupied a privileged (if suspect) space where the assumptions and conventions of print textuality itself (its whole rationalising "Will to Truth") have been tested, even subverted. If "rational" textuality is the prison house of language then poetry is the gymnasium, even the play-room, of language. That remains part of the point of studying it. For it has always resembled a species of *écriture féminine*: it has helped to try out and challenge the implications of attempting to write anything at all. This is even more true of verse written in part dialogue with literary modernism – where the issue of textual presumption and degeneration is of first importance. For which reason, the poetry examined in this book is in an important sense, (diagnostically) the last word about the condition of postmodernity – not the last video image or computer byte or architectural unit or (certainly) the last theory – but the last *word*.

Notes

1. Lyotard writes: "This transition has been under way since at least the end of the 1950s, which for Europe marks the completion of reconstruction." See Jean-François Lyotard, *The Postmodern Condition: A Report on Knowledge*, trans. Geoff Bennington and Brian Massumi with a Foreword by Fredric Jameson (Manchester University Press, 1986), p. 3. Generally I agree with this, although I would wish to place the moment earlier in America.
2. See, for instance, Charles Jencks, *The Language of Post-Modern Architecture* (Academy Editions, 1984); Andreas Huyssen, *After the Great Divide: Modernism, Mass Culture, Postmodernism* (Macmillan, 1986); Brian McHale, *Postmodernist Fiction* (Methuen, 1987); David Harvey, *The Condition of Postmodernity: An Enquiry into the Origins of Cultural Change* (Blackwell, 1988); Steven Connor, *Postmodernist Culture: An Introduction to Theories of the Contemporary* (Blackwell, 1989), *Postmodernism: ICA Documents*, ed. Lisa Appignanesi (Free Associations, 1989).
3. Linda Hutcheon, *A Poetics of Postmodernism: History, Theory, Fiction* (Routledge, 1988).
4. See the titles of Lyotard and Harvey in notes 1 and 2.
5. See Steven Connor, *Postmodernist Culture*, p. 6.
6. See Jean Baudrillard, *Selected Writings*, various translators, ed. Mark Poster (Polity Press, 1988) and *Fatal Strategies*, trans.

Philip Beitchman and W. G. J. Niesluchowski, ed. Jim Fleming (Semiotext(e)/Pluto, 1990).

7. Fredric Jameson, "Postmodernism, or the Cultural Logic of Late Capitalism", *New Left Review*, 146 (1984), pp. 53–92, and his *Postmodernism, or, the Cultural Logic of Late Capitalism* (Verso, 1991).

8. Terry Eagleton, "Capitalism, Modernism and Postmodernism", in *Against the Grain: Essays 1975–1985* (Verso, 1986), pp. 131–48 and his *The Ideology of the Aesthetic* (Basil Blackwell, 1990), pp. 366–415.

9. See Laura Kipnis, "Feminism: The Political Conscience of Postmodernism", in *Universal Abandon: The Politics of Postmodernism*, ed. Andrew Ross (Edinburgh University Press, 1988) pp. 149–66. See also, however, Patricia Waugh's recent comments in *Modern Literary Theory: A Reader*, 2nd edn, ed. Philip Rico and Patricia Waugh (Edward Arnold, 1992), pp. 341–60.

10. See *Selected Writings*, pp. 207–8. On the latter page, he acknowledges "the true revolution which [McLuhan] brought about in media analysis (this has been mostly ignored in France)". Honest words: it has also recently been ignored in Britain, the States and even Canada.

11. Jonathan Miller, *McLuhan* (Fontana/Collins, 1971). In his Introduction Miller writes: "For the purpose of discussion I have deliberately adopted a hostile tone, partly I must admit because I am in almost complete disagreement with the main body of McLuhan's ideas." I was outraged at Miller's treatment of McLuhan when the book first came out: one can only marvel at the editorial policy which allowed this radically uncomprehending account to stand in a generally helpful series. One would also be interested to hear what Dr Miller thinks now of McLuhan's contribution in relation to the present fashion for "Postmodernism".

12. Marshall McLuhan, *The Gutenberg Galaxy* (Routledge and Kegan Paul, 1967); *Understanding Media: The Extensions of Man* (Signet, 1964).

13. See Jeffrey Meyers, *The Enemy: A Biography of Wyndham Lewis* (Routledge & Kegan Paul, 1980), pp. 280–3. McLuhan's magazine COUNTERBLAST was in a dialogical relation with Lewis's BLAST (1914 and 1915), including typographical "probes". McLuhan's book COUNTERBLAST, designed by Harley Parker, was published in Britain by Rapp & Whiting in 1970.

14. Fredric Jameson, *Fables of Aggression: Wyndham Lewis the Modernist as Fascist* (University of California Press, 1979).

15. See, for instance, *Habermas: Autonomy and Solidarity*, ed. Peter Drews (Verso, 1986). See also Jürgen Habermas, *The Philosophical Discourse of Modernity*, trans. Frederick Lawrence (Polity Press, 1987).

16. See Alan Sheridan, *Michel Foucault: The Will to Truth* (Tavistock, 1980), *The Foucault Reader*, ed. Paul Rabinow (Penguin, 1987) and Barry Smart, *Foucault, Marxism and Critique* (Routledge & Kegan Paul, 1985).

17. Thomas Docherty, *After Theory: Postmodernism/Postmarxism* (Routledge, 1990).

18. "The model I have used is that of postmodern architecture, as theorised by Paolo Portoghesi and Charles Jencks and as actualized

by Ricardo Bofill, Aldo Rossi, Robert Stern, Charles Moore, and others" (*A Poetics of Postmodernism*, p. ix); cf. "it was indeed from architectural debates that my own conception of postmodernism ... initially began to emerge" (Jameson, *Postmodernism*, p. 2).

19. Wyndham Lewis's phrase, *Blasting and Bombardiering: An Autobiography (1914–26)* (John Calder, 1982), p. 252; the book was first published in 1937. See also Dennis Brown, *Intertextual Dynamics within the Literary Group – Joyce, Lewis, Pound and Eliot: The Men of 1914* (Macmillan, 1990).

20. In *Time and Western Man* (1927).

21. To James Joyce, 15 November 1926, *The Selected Letters of Ezra Pound 1907–1941*, ed. D. D. Paige (Faber and Faber, 1982), p. 202.

22. Under the thin disguise of Rhoda Hyman, in Wyndham Lewis, *The Roaring Queen*.

23. Williams commented: "I felt at once that it had set me back twenty years" (quoted in Peter Ackroyd, *T. S. Eliot* (Hamish Hamilton, 1984), p. 127).

24. For an account see Dennis Brown, "David Jones and Basil Bunting", *Modern British Poetry*, vol. 2: *1950–1990*, ed. Brian Docherty (Macmillan, forthcoming).

25. *Ibid.*

26. See my *Intertextual Dynamics* for suggestions about Lewis's influence on Beckett.

27. Cf. "It may no longer be possible to deny that postmodernism exists, since the critical debate about postmodernism can be seen partly as the proof of its existence" (Connor, *Postmodernist Culture*, p. 20); and "Postmodernism, postmodern consciousness, may then amount to not much more than theorizing its own condition of possibility" (Jameson, *Postmodernism*, p. ix).

28. *The Times Higher Education Supplement*, 10 August 1990–31 August 1990.

29. Brian McHale, *Postmodernist Fiction*, pp. 9–11.

30. *Ibid.*, pp. 43–58.

31. See Blake Morrison, *The Movement* (Oxford University Press, 1980).

32. See Walter J. Ong, *Orality and Literacy: The Technologizing of the Word* (Methuen, 1982) and Ruth Finnegan, *Oral Poetry: Its Nature, Significance and Social Context* (Cambridge University Press, 1977).

2

W. H. Auden's "Hermes"

With a typical sense of timing (and placement), W. H. Auden signed his "Under Which Lyre"[1] – a commissioned poem – "Harvard, 1946". Both the year and the placing are resonant of the beginnings of the postmodern era: the Second World War was over and Harvard, as much as any institution, can stand as an emblem of that technology-informed intelligence which has energised the "postindustrial" age. Auden's "Tract for the Times" was, in fact, less "reactionary" (as he coyly called it) than prophetic. For it sponsors "precocious Hermes", alluded to in the later "Horae Canonicae" as "any god of crossroads", against monological, masculinist and rationalising Apollo. In a sense, it is itself a "Report on Knowledge". And the poem's playful tone, classical allusions and commitment to the future, as perceived in the present, render it an important aesthetic precursor of the postmodern argument itself. It was not much appreciated in the empiricist England of the coming fifties. Auden, after all, had "betrayed" socialism, wartime England and, indeed, the assumptions of *Scrutiny*. Philip Larkin, in "What has become of Wystan?",[2] ascribed the weaknesses he saw in Auden's later verse to his loss of English rooting. Put another way, however, Auden had internationalised himself by his American exile – and precisely this gave him a sense of the growing "global village" which would characterise postmodernity and rendered him a truly prophetic writer rather than a provincial reactionary.

The word "hermeneutics" is, of course, derived from Hermes – the Greek god who presided at the crossroads of commerce, pilgrimage and knowledge transmission and who, unlike Apollo, was inventor of the lyre – i.e. anti-Apollonian, anti-Platonic poetics. Where Nietzsche sponsored Dionysius as Apollo's opposite (with all the anarchic irresponsibility that implies and which has sometimes infected the intellectual balance of later Parisian disciples), Auden's pairing pits against rationalist power ("He loves to rule, has always done it") less a binary opposition than a personified deconstructor and reinterpreter – both messenger of the gods

15

and patron of "thieves" and "cheats". The last attribution is worth
mentioning since, as "The Sea and the Mirror" (in addition to his
essays) tells us, Auden had a healthy suspicion of the pretensions
of pure aestheticism as well as of the limitations of "Useful
Knowledge". Hence, his proto-poststructuralism promotes tolerant
negotiation rather than attempted demolition. The stance is conflictual yet dialogic:

> Related by antithesis,
> A compromise between us is
>   Impossible;
> Respect perhaps but friendship never:
> Falstaff the fool confronts forever
>   The prig Prince Hal.
>
>   (180)

As we should expect from the choice of Hermes, Auden's later
poetry lacks both the *gravitas* of a Habermas and the intensities of a
Baudrillard: his *jouissance* owes as much to Byron or Edward Lear
as to metaphysical scepticism and the "Hermetic Decalogue" is more
simply funny than subversive – "Thou shalt not answer question-
naires / Or quizzes upon World-Affairs, / Nor with compliance /
Take any test". Auden, whose interest in science was omnivorous,
was not really against testing, or doctoral theses or even "social
science", though he might well have wished them to be conducted
in a less scient*istic* spirit. His tone undermines the intent of both
"decalogue" and logos – for these are authoritarian and Apollon-
ian. In their place he will set the Word as Christ – love not logic,
incarnation not transcendentalism, spirit not letter. Humour
becomes a mode of grace in Auden's mature work. In fact, Erasmus'
In Praise of Folly is a work which springs to mind when savouring
the later, charitable Auden wit.

"The Sea and the Mirror" (signed "August 1942–February 1944")
preceded "Under This Lyre" and anticipates the favouring of
Hermes. Predicated on Prospero's "Shakespearean" renunciation of
the role of patriarchal Magus, the poem might well be read as
Auden's decisive rebuttal of his thirties' role as quasi-Marxist
poetic magician ("Wystan, lone flyer"[3]). Ariel will now be set free;
Prospero will return home to retirement and old age. From a
postmodern perspective, the reworking of Shakespeare's parable
attains a more general dimension: Ariel, the lightning spirit,

represents the potentialities of the "electric age", hitherto confined by the master narratives of postenlightenment modernity; Ariel is now to be liberated – "O, brilliantly, lightly". In the "Postscript", Ariel's lyric asserts his inescapable connection to fleshly, demotic, marginalised and suppressed Caliban. Reversing Eliot's patrician fear of Sweeney, Auden hymns that new magic whose "devotion" will dazzle and entertain democratic "drab mortality". Under the auspices of Hermes, cosmic dialogism becomes immediate reality at the speed of near light: "reply/...I" (*sic*). It reminds one of television satellite link-up chat-shows.

It has been noticed not only that Auden's Prospero admits guilt with respect to Caliban ("my impervious disgrace") but that what Caliban has to say (and he gets the lion's share of discourse) in many ways replicates what Auden's Prospero says about the limitations of art and the seriousness of life's "tremendous journey". Caliban is made the Kierkegaardian spokesman (through Jamesian pastiche) of the ultimate signified/signifier which is the goal of the leap of faith: "the real Word which is our only *raison d'être*". Caliban represents an early instance of the centralisation of the marginalised and well precedes instances of the same phenomenon in such texts as Jean Rhys's *The Wide Sargasso Sea*, Tom Stoppard's *Rosencrantz* and *Guildenstern are Dead* or J. M. Coeetze's *Foe*. In Shakespeare's play, of course, Caliban is less a disinherited native son than the son of the witch of Algiers – yet he remains "other" to the Europeans. Auden adapts the idea that Prospero taught his slave language to the ultimately postcolonial scenario where an unrooted coloured subject appropriates the Mandarin discourse of some "Great Tradition" to better the conclusions of his academic mentor and offer a more satisfying "restored relation" than the plot of *The Tempest* provided.

"Our incorrigible staginess" is a key theme in the poem – as, under the concept of "simulacrum" or "language game", it is a major motif of the postmodern argument. Auden takes his own key from the self-consciously "theatrical" ending in *The Tempest* itself. It is debatable how far Auden was influenced by Brecht's ideas on "alienation"[4] – yet there is something generally Brechtian in the characterisation of the Preface: "The Stage Manager to the Critics". Auden's "commentary" is also prefaced by a quotation from Emily Brontë and the actual Preface concludes with a kind of Keatsian or Wilson Knight summary of the Shakespearean message ("the silence ripeness, / And the ripeness all") which suggests that the evoked "Critics" are less first-night newspaper hacks than the developing practitioners of literary criticism – whom Auden, as campus lecturer would have known all about. The Stage Manager, unlike, say, F. R. Leavis or Yvor Winters, emphasises the circus, Magic Circle and pantomime aspects of the aesthetic – in short, literature as a species of carnival. A shirt-sleeves deconstructionist, he knows no metaphor can fill "the lion's mouth".

Prospero's farewell to Ariel also acknowledges the "magical" nature of art. Yet it further recognises the "mirror" uses of the aesthetic and suggests that "the way of truth" may be a mode of "silence" rather than some species of either Socratic dialectic or Aristotelian monologism. Prospero's speech is interrupted and concluded by skilful and ironic lyrics (again Brecht springs to mind, though sometimes Dryden too). This is a more chastened Prospero than that at the end of *The Tempest* – and one profoundly "postmodernised" through the relaxed, playful free verse.

There follow the voices of "The Supporting Cast" – *sotto voce*. Antonio comes first, as another self-confessed failure of Prospero: "I tempted Antonio into treason". Antonio's main motive is to deny the validity of Prospero's magically wrought new order. He sees it merely as a "grouping" – a power structure as artificial as the means used to effect it. He sceptically rejects Prospero's claim that he has renounced his powers, pointing out that both wand and books could easily be reclaimed. The very fact that Antonio stands "alone", refusing reconciliation – as he appears to do in *The Tempest* – will make his brother wish somehow to "charm" him back into his "circle". He represents Prospero as the eternal adult, unable to return to innocence or peace and inextricably complicit in the new social ordering he has conjured into existence. Prospero constitutes the oppressor, whatever reconcilation he feels he may have effected: a symbolisation, we may feel, of Western power, he is implicated in the plight of all that has been suppressed, marginalised or distorted in order to achieve his aim. For all his cry of "I am I", Auden's Antonio reminds us less, in the end, of Milton's Satan (who acts rather than broods) than of the position of, say, Michel Foucault: as Terry Eagleton has observed of the latter: "What is objectionable is *regime as such*".[5]

Auden is both less totalising and more charitable than Foucault in his representation of power and powerlessness. Antonio is given his say, as Caliban will be, but so are a variety of "losers and winners". It is notable, however, that the end lyrics of each of these centre-section contributions allude to the somewhat baleful presence of Antonio – burning, toasting, talking, playing, wearing, sailing, fighting, laughing and dancing, always "alone". Ferdinand's sonnet follows Antonio's intervention and celebrates both his love for Miranda and the higher "tenderness" seen here as "light". Ferdinand makes it explicit that although he is entranced with his lot – marriage and the kingdom – he does not regard Prospero's arrangement as perfect in itself. There is a Platonic[6] and Augustinian emphasis in his evocation of "The Right Required Time" and "Place". The City of God is both immanent in and transcendent of even the best political ordering – it is never identical with it. This theme is typical of the later, postMarxist Auden and looks forward to what Caliban will say about "the real Word" in the longest section of the poem.

Stephano represents the banal sensuality of much postmodernity – a man whose belly is his god and who negotiates the grotesque material surpluses of the "first world" between the bottle and the "loo" (a kind of proto-lager-lout). In this, he is self-confessedly a divided self, split between flesh and spirit, signifier and signified. Between the "thing" and "name", he is helplessly lost in the realm of the Baudrillardian "simulacrum" – "inert", as he finally confesses. Yet what is embodied here is also the material plenty, with all its invitations to excess, which the postmodern West has inherited from the materialistic "magic" of modernity. Prospero's miracle has merely confirmed Stephano in his own excesses by not leaving him to starve on the island but returning him to a "modernising" Milan.

Gonzalo's tone is less "lost" but perhaps more rueful, and certainly more contemplative. In Shakespeare, Gonzalo is characterised by nobility and gentleness and he lives to bless the marriage of Ferdinand and Miranda. Nevertheless, for all that he furnished Prospero and his daughter with provisions and the crucial books, he was also complicit in the circumstances of the banishment, with all its maritime perils. So Auden makes him content with his "prediction" yet aware he is not "justified". He doubted the "Absurd" and finally lacked love, he says. He also "froze / Vision into an idea" – a bit like Yeats's version of John Locke: in allegorical terms (and all these figures are allegorical representations rather than realistic characters), he might stand for the contradictory beneficence and mechanisation of Enlightenment thinking – where, as it were, Prospero becomes the Einstein of the postmodern, inaugurating an era where an older notion of Mystery could be reasserted in the ruins of a narrow rationality and *realpolitik*. Certainly, Gonzalo here applauds the restitution of "subjective passion" and affirms "The Already There". In some respects, this figure is less a representation of Shakespeare's counsellor than a personification of the modern era – the repentant political "interferer" now in the "Age of Anxiety". The cautionary gravity of his self-confession contrasts strongly with the fripperies of Adrian and Francisco who follow merely to glitter either as "sunbeams" or "goldfish".

Alonso's speech is directed to his son, Ferdinand. It constitutes advice concerning what Auden's publisher, T. S. Eliot, had called the "Difficulties of a Statesman". Behind it, one senses (as often in Auden), a lost Edwardian order ("the park so green, / So many well-fed pigeons") which has been shattered by the "convulsions" of twentieth century world war. The "temperate city" is not for later Auden the possible "just city" of "Spain" – the communistic Madrid of the "heart" – but an actuality, in the incarnate world, never far from Dante's Lake of Cocytus where fire and ice meet in stupendous conjunction. For Alonso, kingship is an existential commitment, set against but aware of the all-levelling horizon of the "cold deep"; it cannot be ideal but it is necessary. It is also lonely: no help can be expected "from others" and it constitutes a tightrope walked in the pursuit of "Justice". The kingdom is powered by "synchronised clocks" and discourse about "Progress", yet it is narrowly proximate to both sea and waste land where all privilege of rule is tested and annihilated. This is the realm of actual, as opposed to Utopian, politics – and Auden's lines allow no access to either the tyrant's discourse of necessity nor the victim's accusatory hysteria. They are the product of an honest writer who had toyed with the metadiscourses of theoretical totalisation and acknowledged, in the end, that: "unattractive and shallow as one may feel so many liberals to be, how rarely on any concrete issues does one find the liberal position to be the wrong one".[7]

Alonso offers his advice, reconciles himself to the "humming sail" of return and rejoices in his new acquaintance with love and peace – as he anticipates death.

The song of "Master and Boatswain" immediately deflates the *engagé* solemnity of Alonso (and, throughout, the poem exploits dissolves, collage and interfaces). These men are the sturdy operatives of the modern voyage into the unknown; wastrels both –

and, hence, anarchically outside the patriarchal order even while exploiting it – they both use and are used by the black market economy of sexual supply and demand. So their boisterous song celebrates the dubious charms of Margery and Kate, at the expense of marriageable Meg and Marion and admits to playing at domesticity when they have no intention of joining the middle class or any other order. They drink, copulate and take refuge in sleep. Next day the "compass" will call them again: they are somewhat idealised rogues – perhaps not so far from Derek Jarman's dancing tars in his film version of *The Tempest.*

Sebastian's contribution comes in the form of a sestina – an elaborate and self-contained poetic form where, before the recapitulatory "envoy", six key end terms are reworked in different line positions six times. Stan Smith, whose study of Auden speaks to the condition of postmodernity (and who is particularly good on valuation terms in *The Sea and the Mirror*), has written: "The sestina works its changes upon the key words as if to remind [Sebastian] of that closed circle from which only Failure and Exposure free him".[8] This seems right: in *The Tempest* Sebastian had been plotting to repeat the act of usurpation, on the island itself, by killing his own brother (Alonso, King of Naples), along with Antonio. He now sees that the "sword" can never entail legitimacy. This is the song of a man who has "come through" – as Antonio has not. Sebastian finally accepts that: "Right Here is absolute and needs no crown". His version recycles the differential terms which motivated his villainy, but it also points to a "Now" where swords must be suffered not used. He offers his repentant dance of words to the reader's attention.

Trinculo contributes a quasi-Shakespearean song to express the clown as type. He is the opposite of Stephano, the sensual man locked in his appetite. Trinculo, by contrast, can never plant his feet on the "solid world". His act is a form of defence ("dreams") to preserve him from the "terror"that haunts him. For this very reason, he is socially useful – even loved after a fashion. His jokes serve to liberate others, too, from their groundlessness in both matter and terror. "History" and "love" become mere signifiers – his "flock of words" are themselves simulacra, as insubstantial as the television comedian or game host: merely "wild images".

If Trinculo is entrapped in signification, Miranda is caught in the mirror world of human love. However, there are no Lacanian, psychic complexities involved in this version of the "mirror stage".

For the reflectionism of love is sung here as release from both witchy venom and the phallus as threat: it means the marital bond, as natural as hill by sea or children dancing – and, indeed, the dance of children is what it looks toward. Miranda's song is in the form of a villanelle – five three-line stanzas and a final quatrain, using only two rhymes, with the first and third lines of stanza one repeated alternatively in succeeding stanzas until the final couplet. The very elaborate matching qualities, repetitions and even artificiality embody the magical attraction between the two lovers and the quasi-narcissistic entanglement of the two in each other. However, if Miranda is fixated on Ferdinand's awakening kiss, she does not forget Gonzalo, the "Ancient" who prayed for her and later for them. It is fitting that the voices of the "Supporting Cast" should end with Miranda's song of love: for hers is not the discourse of power, but that, simply, of the incarnate future. In this most male of plays, her womanly "magic" is, indeed, her own.

Caliban would normally be regarded as part of the minor cast rather than as either protagonist (Prospero) or antagonist (Antonio). In *The Sea and the Mirror* he is chief spokesperson – and, unlike the stage manager, he speaks not to the critics but directly to the audience. It is interesting that Auden, when a schoolboy, had taken the part of Caliban in a production of *The Tempest*, to considerable effect.[9] His promotion of Caliban, in the poem, is itself a *coup de théâtre* rather than a Blakean overthrow of established order. As already noted, what Caliban says is an embroidery on Prospero's privileging of life over art rather than a rebuttal of what his master had stood for – and it all comes filtered through the mannered cadences of Henry James. In this way, Auden enacts, in his language, the point about art's unreliability (as artifice): for fictive self-consciousness, through radical pastiche, has rarely been given such "serious" prominence.

Through magisterial parodic elaboration, Caliban begins by establishing his initial point and the foundation of all he has to say: nearly thirty years before Roland Barthes' essay on the question, he announces "The Death of the Author". The audience (intentionalists to a man?) are envisaged as wishing to applaud "our so good, so great, so dead author" and enquiring of him what the production has been "*about*". Logos, the "all-explaining master", cannot, alas, appear, Caliban intimates, so *he* will have to do. In fact, "our native Muse" is, anyway, open to "*tout le monde*" and, hence, inherently susceptible to the viewer's own interpretation or "Reader Response".

Defending the ways of the "gracious goddess" at length, Caliban eventually proceeds to an extraordinarily extended sentence on the less fortunate, who cannot attend the performance, which sounds like a parody of Foucault written by Beckett's Pozzo. It begins grandiosely: "we should not be sitting here now ... " and ends "in damp graves" (155) and is one of the highlights of the speech. However, Caliban is nothing if not prolix: he proceeds to demand the whereabouts of Ariel (fearing the effect of the "poetic" on the real – and making Ariel's emprisoned "call for help" sound like the life myths of Robert Lowell, John Berryman or Sylvia Plath), to warn would-be magicians of the future and to uphold unassimilable experience against art's rage for order.

Caliban defines himself as of the same stuff as the audience – "all too solid flesh" (161). He addresses us "on behalf of Ariel and myself". He will not answer questions because we already know the answers; we all have our tickets on the journey of life and though we are always prone to regress ("Pick me up, uncle"[10]), we know, in ourselves, that "this" is it. Despite statistical methods and the variety of human activities (169) – and here he foreshadows Lucky rather than Pozzo – we still deceive ourselves chronically and the performance is about to end. So Auden's extraordinary spokesman sums up: there is no way out, God is our only *raison d'être*; at most, life – as art itself – can offer only "figurative signs" and through these we can in fact, believe in Mercy – in which, alone, we can be reconciled. It is a *tour de force* – the more so by its postmodern indirectness and playfulness which always alludes to higher truth. Auden we know, thought it about the best thing he had ever done:[11] one can see why; apart from the extraordinary execution, the method is prophetically fertile.

However, there is still the "Postscript" in which Ariel woos Caliban, echoed by the prompter. This is a fine lyric which looks back to Shakespeare through Lawes and Dryden. Yet its message may be more postmodern than the comparison suggests. Ariel and Caliban represent binary oppositions, yet such contrastive partialities may come together in the sigh of desire for the ultimate signified. Magical art is in love with life, but the meaning of both remains open. They are hymned as positive and negative where both need some absolute "earthing". Ariel sings and such is his lightness, the speed of response, that he sings, in a sense, the era electric.

Seen from the present stage in the construction of postmodernism, Auden's achievement in "The Sea and the Mirror" is extraordinary.

The major devices are already there: the "quotationality" of playing off the master text; the glossalalia of radical (and unresolved) dialogism; allegory as mode, parody and pastiche, self-conscious fictionality, self-referentiality, "serious" play and the theatrical reworking of such historic verse forms as the sonnet, the sestina and the villanelle – they are all deployed. The "Commentary" is a "maggot", in John Fowles' sense – yet in the ordinary sense, perhaps, too. For Auden's masterpiece (as much "miss" as "master"?) is a parasitic infestation of a canonised work: a deconstructive decoding which also recodes. It is also, like much recent poetry, a diffusion of rationalist hubris, a subversion of all power systems and an evocation of a higher order and meaning beyond the realm of earthly revels. This maggot dreams to be a butterfly.

"Horae Canonicae" (1949–54) is a later poetic sequence which expresses Auden's religious apprehension of postmodernity more directly. The chief motif here is to "recycle" the canonical hours of prayer as a means both of expressing and placing the world of "synchronised clocks": Auden offers the cyclical, liturgical pattern as contemporaneous code. The existential anguish of Kierkegaard and the social concern of the Niebuhrs are here conjoined – as in the thirties' poems Marx and Freud had been. Yet the tone is never portentous, for all the evocation of the "cement of blood": this is true in each of the seven sections but is even more a product of the loose, collagistic nature of the sequence as a whole. Whether artfully formal or deceptively relaxed, the verse is self-consciously artifice even as it "mirrors" the realities of the diurnal round. The one-day time scheme, recalling *Ulysses*, *Mrs Dalloway* and even the clocks in *The Waste Land*, provides a somewhat neoclassical scaffolding to the contrastive meditations. If it constantly alludes to the "crucified god",[12] the poem is an affirmation of the incarnate world which such sacrifice, paradoxically, renders worth living. Our "dear old bag of a democracy" is blessed as "the green world temporal".

"Prime" celebrates both waking up and the Adamic quality of even the modern world. It cannily evokes the disorientation of the average early morning – the reclaiming of an "adjacent arm" as one's own. In fact, the whole section – one elaborated sentence in each of three stanzas – is centrally about owning oneself and taking responsibility (in Robert Duncan's sense too – the "ability to respond") for one's existential being and one's commitment in the whole world. The Freudian realm of dream's "rebellious fronde" is abandoned as the self reawakes into a name and a history. The marginal placing, "the "fishing village", is centralised as a node in the social whole where "routine" is resumed but personal "dying" will also be involved.

"Terse" elaborates the moment of setting off for work – even if only round and round the poet's garden. Allegorical figures – hangman, judge, the "Big Ones", "the girls" – are loosely utilised to suggest a variagated typical day whose "machinery" will be started up for another day's work. The second stanza evokes what Wyndham Lewis called "inferior religions", yet here the personal "image" of an image is neither mere "shadow" nor scandalous simulacrum but the lot of ordinary experience, finally guaranteed by Platonic and Dantesque "Law". The day is still potentiality, yet already the answer of prayer is immanent in the unfolding of flux. Thanks to the contemporary world's "victim", there will be a "good Friday". The section moves from the comic banale ("shaking paws with his dog") to the affirmation of "miracle".

"Sext", set at noon, is divided into three sections, the verse casually split into cellular, unrhymed couplets. The first section praises practical skills – "that eye-on-the-object look" – and the patron saints who preside over them, as opposed to "appetitive goddesses" like Venus or Diana. Auden explicitly commits himself to the makers of the modern "city". The second section, concentrating on the mouth as the first does on the eye, also apostrophises modernity as a mode of "incarnation" and compares it favourably with a caricature of "primitivism" as *patois* and inbreeding. The third section evokes the crowd, in a vein similar to Elias Canetti. Yet this crowd is above all witness to the crucifixion – Eliot's crowd on London Bridge refigured here as "brothers" capable of worship. The passion of Christ is made to seem relevant not only to the Kierkegaardian "Knight of faith" but also to the many-headed multitude. Auden is fully in the tradition of "Christian Socialism".

"Nones" is a seven-stanza meditation on the awesome similarity in the *difference* separating "will" and "kill". It accepts the writer's own complicity in the structure of power, including its sometimes lethal consequences, in a way most theorisations of the postmodern do not. This discourse is authentically *engagé*. Toward the end the tone and rhythm of Eliot's *Four Quartets* is evident and three Madonnas preside over a world where the dreadful has already happened – again. The penultimate stanza exploits a nightmare scenario through quasi-cinematic means, culminating in the room, lit by a single bulb, where each of us meets our own Double – and is not recognised. The last stanza constitutes a hymn to the natural, biological processes which underlie and sustain the human melodrama: "At the right moment, essential fluids / Flow to renew exhausted cells ... ". This is a holistic conclusion evoking a finally poignant deer – but not excluding the comicality of "smug hens". As often, the Auden *caritas* comes spiced with good humour.

"Vespers" is perhaps the most strikingly unusual section of the poem: the most polarised by attitudinal oppositionality and the one most, therefore, in need of Hermetic negotiation between "different fibs". The crucial encounter, in the "civil twilight", is set up rather like Eliot's confrontation with the "familiar compound ghost" in "Little Gidding". But here the other is not some "dead master" but an opposite – and so, probably, a Double. The persona owns himself to be an Aquarian against the antagonist's Scorpio, but the double trouble of Auden's own career – Utopianism versus incarnationalism – comprehends both positions. It is "New Jerusalem" versus Eden, as the poet seeks to find accommodation between urgent opposites. The fantasy of chefs as "cucumber-cool machine minders" speaks powerfully to the service industries of postmodernity, as both "rational virtues" and "compulsive rituals" foreshadow the continuing turmoil of Eastern Europe, while the rickets-smitten child reminds us of a "Third World" at once postmodern and premodern. The conclusion speaks of our grounding in bloodshed, looking forward to Geoffrey Hill's most striking early poem.[13] Auden's Hermetic mysteries ground the *via negativa* in the signature of an all-too-physical killing.

Where "Vespers" tends toward aphorism (that "electric age" subversion of explanation),[14] "Compline" represents verse meditation, again in somewhat Eliotic mood. Now the day is over – or nearly so. The poet fails to see "either plot / Or meaning" in the diurnal unfolding: it is beyond neoAristotelian *logocentrism*. However, Auden uses quite abstract language to confess language's own limitations and announces the return to the "unwashed tribe of wishes" of a night's dreaming. He queries postmodern signification in-itself:

Can poets (can men in television)
Be saved?

(231)

It is a good question. Auden (charitably) invokes the plight of "all poor s–o–bs" and concludes in prayer for reconciliation "about the abiding tree".

"Lauds" is a deliberately "archaic", hence self-consciously artificial, conclusion. It is somewhere between "camp" and lyrical anamnesis. Two-line units vary a limited number of lines in fresh combination, followed always by the refrain: "*In solitude, for company*". This refrain perhaps memorialises the fate of the textual poet within the new "global village". The poetic "art and sullen craft" remains a lonely, marginalised activity – yet it seeks to speak to a changed world with the old (prose-discourse suppressed) magic of rhythm and rhyme. With the *insouciance* of an expert registrator of the present, it reinvests the textual banalities of the past with a knowing "folk" dimension:

God bless the Realm, God bless the People.
(232)

Rarely can such a line have been so "meant" and "unmeant" at the same time – the verbalisation near fatuous, the sentiment imperative. Auden's "Horae" ends in an "ora"; even postmodern hours can only be really "ours" through intercession.

What Auden's later verse alerts us to, long before the construction of postmodernism as critical category, is the failure of both Freudian and Marxist master narrative, the poverty of mere social realism and the virtue not only of dialogism, irony and allegory but also of deliberate religious belief as a perspective on the contemporary. The latter phenomenon was much in evidence during the genuinely "revolutionary" *événements* of 1989 when world-wide television showed ritualistic candles pitted against "demystifying" machine guns as the East European quasi-Marxist narrative unravelled in carnivalesque popular protest. Auden, who sponsored carnival long before Bakhtin became a theory-sponsored entrée to the wisdom of Rabelais or Dostoevsky, would surely have approved such a phenomenon – even as he would mistrust any potentialities of religious dogmatism or nationalist bigotry. John G. Blair has suggested of "Under Which Lyre" that: "the incongruous jumble of religiously serious principles and apparent trivia helps to create a sense that Hermes stands for an all-embracing outlook on life".[15] That sounds right. Later Auden avoided theoretical totalisation, even in spheres he believed in strongly: he was for dramatic exploration of the issues and playful dialogism with the intelligent reader.

His pursuit of this has involved the deployment of many of the devices now said to be characteristic of postmodern aesthetics: in this, one might suggest, he was very much a pioneer. His use of allegory, for instance (rather than the modernist symbol), is typical. So too is the use of "quotationality" – whether from the Anglo-Saxon or Greek worlds – and the ability to mix low forms (ballad or song) and high forms (quasi-epic or meditative). The subject, in all Auden's poetry, is characteristically decentred while the propensity towards irony, humour and play foreshadows the postmodern norm. In addition, as "high" poet, Auden specialises in a trope which speaks back memorably to the postmodern rhetoric of the slogan, headline or sound bite – namely the trope of aphorism. Auden appropriates the code form of commercial information to reinvest it as a mode of deep probe. Auden's aphorisms tend to be ethically responsible and spiritually profound: "To your faults be true" (174), "In our morale must lie our strength" (182), "The barbed wire runs through the abolished city" (193), "For without a cement of blood (it must be human, it must be innocent) no secular wall will safely stand" (229). Though sometimes on the brink of cliché, indeed sometimes perhaps because of that, Auden's lines are among the most accessible, memorable and hortatory of the era. In an environment of junk phrases, Auden used a more permanent rhetoric to ground the contemporary in the eternal and promote what Hans Küng[16] has called" signs of a productive, forward-looking change towards a new postmodern overall constellation."

Notes

1.   For easy accessibility, all quotations are taken from W. H. Auden, *Selected Poems*, ed. Edward Mendelson (Faber, 1979). "Under Which Lyre" is published on pp. 178–83.
2.   Philip Larkin, "What Has Become of Wystan?", in *Required Writing: Miscellaneous Pieces 1955–1982* (Faber, 1983).
3.   "Look west, Wystan, lone flyer, birdman, my bully boy!", C. Day Lewis's salute in "The Magnetic Mountain", *Collected Poems 1954* (Jonathan Cape, 1970), p. 97.
4.   See Humphrey Carpenter, *W. H. Auden: A Biography* (Allen and Unwin, 1981), p. 85.
5.   Terry Eagleton, *The Ideology of the Aesthetic* (Blackwell, 1990), p. 385.
6.   For a consideration of later Auden's use of Platonism, see Daphne Turner, "Auden and Platonism" in *Platonism and the English Literary*

Imagination, ed. Anna Baldwin and Sarah Hutton (Cambridge University Press, forthcoming).

7. Quoted by Humphrey Carpenter, *W. H. Auden*, p. 421.
8. Stan Smith, *W. H. Auden* (Blackwell, 1985), p. 158.
9. See Humphrey Carpenter, *W. H. Auden*, p. 41. It is interesting with respect to Auden's early sponsoring of Caliban, that Doris Summet's account of the South American, magical-realist "boom" includes the phrase: "Caliban could at last possess his kingdom". "Irresistible Romance: the Foundational Fictions of Latin America", in Homi K. Bhabha (ed.), *Nation and Narration* (Routledge, 1990), p. 71. In this book, overall, postcolonial and postmodern writings are seen to be intertwined.
10. It is possible Auden is playing off the poignant "Carry me along, taddy, like you done through the toy fair!" on the last page of James Joyce's *Finnegans Wake* (Faber, 1975), p. 628.
11. See Humphrey Carpenter, *W. H. Auden*, p. 328.
12. His understanding seems similar to that in Jürgen Moltmann, *The Crucified God* (Student Christian Movement, 1974).
13. "There is no bloodless myth will hold" (Geoffrey Hill, "Genesis", *Collected Poems* (King Penguin, 1985), p. 16).
14. Auden himself commented: "The aphorist does not argue or explain: he asserts...It is for the reader to decide...whether an aphorism be true or false" (quoted by Humphrey Carpenter, *W. H. Auden*, p. 401). In McLuhan's terminology the aphorism constitutes "cool" (participatory) not "hot" discourse.
15. John G. Blair, *The Poetic Art of W. H. Auden* (Princeton University Press, 1965), p. 87.
16. Hans Küng, *Global Responsibility: In Search of a New World Ethic*, trans. John Bowden (Student Christian Movement, 1991), p. 4.

3

Allen Ginsberg's "America"

Ginsberg's two most celebrated poems, "Howl" and "Kaddish", are both love songs and requiems of a kind – the first for a "buddy" (Carl Solomon) and, by extension, for a generation, the second for his mother "Naomi" and the experience of immigration into the New World. However, his poetic *oeuvre* overall (as represented in *Collected Poems 1947–1980*)[1] registers a larger subject – "America" as contemporary hyperreal experience – and sponsors, as poetic mode, the long-lined, psalmic and prophetic "open field" text as a means of expressing "Americanness". In terms of modern Western poetry, Blake, Whitman, William Carlos Williams and Pound were particularly pertinent to the construction of Ginsberg's vision and agglutinative style. Yet diachronous "influence" seems less important here than synchronous *relevance*. For Ginsberg's democratic, all-inclusive rhetoric, attuned to highly committed "antennae" of consciousness, effects a vision and mode of expression far more significant than any particular poem or poems he has written. For instance, it is difficult to think about the more ambitious lyrics of, say, Bob Dylan, John Lennon or Van Morrison without the Ginsbergian precedent.

In general, Ginsberg tried out and tested the implications of an "End of History"[2] thesis from within the grotesque torsions of the Cold War. His characteristic themes – the entropy of corporate materialism, the repression of sexual and spiritual desire, the nightmare scenarios of nuclear exchange and the increasing pollution of the planet – were proleptic at the time and are mandatory now. And his characteristically unshackled discourse – paratactical, alogical, comprehensive, insistently rhythmic, laid back, dialogical, ironic and passionate – both replicated "electric age" modes of communication and gave them a human dimension and voice.

The poem "America", from *Howl and Other Poems*,[3] is a useful text through which to begin assessment of Ginsberg's representation of the postmodern. Dated with the precision of a weather forecast ("Berkeley, January 17, 1956"), "America" threads a destabilising irony into the expansive, Whitmanesque line unit. Its almost deliberate casualness is intentionally offensive to verse tradition- alists – then or after. Yet the quasi-diary registration is scarcely more radical than Joyce's conclusion to *Portrait of the Artist*[4] and, indeed, the consistent focus of address ("America I ...") gives it a coherence beyond Stephen Dedalus' random reflections. In very general terms, this is a "Confessional" poem: the personal is the political and vice versa. Hence, the "I" construction is able to claim a representative postmodern status despite its "Beat" peculiarity: "I'm sick of your insane demands" or "I am talking to myself again". The ideologically interpellated[5] "free self" drifts between *"Time Magazine"* and "television set", \$2.27 and 25,000 "mental institutions", the Wobblies and the atomic bomb – the USA, India, France and Tangier. "I am America", but in the sense that America constitutes a margin ("Berkeley Public Library") in a global web where Fordism and post-Fordist information technology call the shots. Both psychoanalysis and variants of Marxism are invoked: Sacco and Vanzetti share space with "Uncle Max"; Russia and China constitute an aggregated "Other" which is (paradoxically?) obsessed with possessing American "filling-stations". At which point, the split subject appropriates Indian pow-wow palaver ("Her needs ...", "Him make ...") to re-establish "America" as a simul- acrum of roots, historical struggle and identity-in-depth. It is a persona John Berryman will reuse extensively as African–American counter-voice in *Dream Songs*.

The poem "America" constitutes a peculiarly postmodern conjunction of textual and oral[6] modes within an already com- prehensive electronic culture. It is clearly designed to be read aloud or chanted – no doubt, initially in the City Lights Bookshop, San Francisco. Behind the poem lie the mandatory voices of the Jewish Major Prophets; beyond it, as it were, shimmer the video images of pop electronics and the sonorous tonalities of the electric guitar. It constitutes a literary "Born in the USA" some thirty years before Bruce Springsteen's lyric rocked around the world. In fact, this poem – as all of Ginsberg in that era – registers a reemergence into print textuality of the repressed primal rhythms of oral culture, riding on electrified jazz and blues. It re-energises the muted tom- tom beat which lurks under *The Waste Land*'s mandarin allusions and confirms the "breaking" of the pentameter which was Pound's declared poetic springboard. It is postmodern most specifically in its exploitation of the liberational possibilities of the modernist line and its establishment of a vatic stammer as one expression of the new "NEW":

> Are you going to let your emotional life be run by
>   Time Magazine?
> I'm obsessed by Time Magazine.
> I read it every week ... .
>
>   (147)

The America of the poem is less an empirical place than a mind zone. Ginsberg's selected experiences are here projected into a contemporary simulacrum which could be recognised and appropriated by the *avant-garde* West at large. The almost immediate translatability of *Howl and Other Poems* testifies to the poetry's inherent ability to speak to and for the "electric age". It is "depthless" in the sense that the poetic texture is a kind of verbal silk-screen where global imagery flickers insubstantially, irony overlays agony and the ghosts of old ideological arguments flit acros the imaginative terrain. Yet this need not detract from the poem's significance – it truly inscribes salient realities: what is under question is not significance but "seriousness",[7] here denominated as a *Time Magazine* slogan. In place of this, "America" offers arguably more important values – for example, relevance, honesty and vision. Here humour becomes an important factor in the registration of a postmodern America where puritanical earnestness (packaged like peas) and monological rhetoric (in the service of social power) were a great part of the problem. The poem is dialogical in that it speaks *to*, as well as of, the contemporary USA – talking back, also, to its immediate informational modes. And long before the recognised construction of a Gay Rights movement, it uses comedic sexual transgression as a way of getting in the last word: "America I'm putting my queer shoulder to the wheel".

"I saw..."; there could scarcely be a more overt, Johannine and apocalyptic declaration to begin Ginsberg's founding, major poem – "Howl". And what *is* seen here *is*, again, the postmodern America-of-the-mind. The function of the seer is collective rather than individual and the seeing is a mode of bardic vision rather than a manipulation of some objectivising gaze. The two come together in the generational project the poem apostrophises:

who dreamt and made incarnate gaps in Time & Space through
images juxtaposed, and trapped the archangel of the soul
between 2 visual images and joined the elemental verbs and
set the noun and dash of consciousness together jumping with
sensation of Pater Omnipotens Aeterna Deus ... .

(130)

If the aesthetic method has its origins in artists such as Pound or Max
Ernst, it also anticipates the advent of video culture, though with a
religious intensity rarely found in the televisual sequence. Whereas
with experimental film or video the spectre of the simulacrum
haunts the medium and message, here it is the invoked world that is
hyperreal: walls communicate "the Terror", advertisers emit
"nitroglycerine shrieks", radio is accused of "hypnotism". In a bold
preLaingian move, the social sphere is represented as insane, while
the outsiders – "the best minds of my generation" – are the figures
who assert "Absolute Reality" – through the eyes of "Plotinus Poe St
John of the Cross", "Mohammedan angels" or "tender Buddha".
World religions are here brought together to shore up the poet's
vision of a postmodern social sphere without substance or meaning.

The contemporary waste land is named in the second section as
"Moloch". Moloch (or Molech) was a Canaanite idol which consumed the children offered to it – and so does "America" consume
its younger generation in the poem. The predicated "zone" encapsulates the economic and political realities of postmodernity:

Moloch whose love is endless oil and stone! Moloch whose soul
is electricity and banks! Moloch whose poverty is the specter of
genius! Moloch whose fate is a cloud of sexless hydrogen!
Moloch whose name is the Mind!

(131)

Which Mind? Surely what is condemned here is a denomination of
what Michel Foucault will call the "Will to Truth" – the scientific–
technological, masculinist and imperialising spread of power
through knowledge across the entire globe. Ginsberg focuses on the
human "fall-out" involved:

... Solitude! Filth! Ugliness! Ashcans and unobtainable dollars!
Children screaming under the stairways! Boys sobbing in
armies! Old men weeping in the parks!

Moloch is a self-generating industrial–military complex which is wholly oblivious to its effects on any kind of planetary life form. Yet it is also represented as a manifestation of patriarchal, phallic hubris: "granite cocks! monstrous bombs!" Again, this is some ten to fifteen years before the consolidating resistance of post-Second World War feminism really challenged masculinist culture in its varied manifestations. "Howl" claims, overtly, to be prophetic (in the double sense of the term)[8] and, indeed it *is*. Informed, but unentranced, by Marxist narratives of modern history, it tells the present and imminent truth of postmodernity from its position of best advantage in the fifties – not Paris, but the American west coast.

However, the third and culminatory section of the poem invokes "America" in Rockland. Once again, the radio is representative of the "electric age" – to whose messages of neurotic disaster the poet transmits back solidarity "on the same dreadful typewriter". Both bard and addressee are interconnected on an imaginative plane where the psychic and political are inextricably interwoven: "where we hug and kiss the United States under our bedsheets, the United States that coughs all night and won't let us sleep." Humour, "murder", innocence and insanity conjoin in "faculties of the skull" that are simultaneously mapping centres for the worlds of Utica, Long Island and the Bronx. The poem moves to culmination as religious and political defiance: it also ends in Romantic fantasy, remaking the USA experience as a fable of return and reconciliation:

> ... in my dreams you walk dripping from a sea-journey
> on the highway across America in tears to
> the door of my cottage in the Western night.

> (133)

The somewhat mysteriously named "Death to Van Gogh's Ear!" is typical of Ginsberg's anti-materialist registration of postmodern "America". Its second line reads "Money has reckoned the soul of America" – its last: "Money against Eternity! and eternity's strong mills grind out vast papers of illusion." If the "papers of illusion" are understood primarily as dollar bills, then Ginsberg's early critique of postmodernity concerns its economic misappropriation and maldistribution of planetary resources through hyperreal market mechanisms controlled by "Owners! Owners! Owners!", masquerading as an illusory "creation"[9] of wealth. The "End of

History" is already inscribed here as a synchronic web interconnecting "Australia", "Tanganyika", "Asia", "Kra", Puerto Rico, "Russia" and "Texas", supported by "nerve gas over the radio" as "propaganda" and infusing all politics as a chimerical racket monitored by "monsters" and set against destiny, divinity and eternity.

Ginsberg's still-contemporaneous critique was written in 1957 – two months after the launch of the first sputnik and before Richard Nixon was arguing in Moscow the American superiority in making washing-machines! It was also written in Paris – eleven years before those *événements* which finally shook French intellectuals out of their Marxian rigidity. Where then lay Ginsberg's point of purchase on the system? About this he is romantically, perhaps overconfidently, assured: "Poet is Priest". That is how the poem opens; what it means in modern terms is elaborated even before McLuhan's similar formulation: "I am the defense early warning system" – an updating of Pound's idea of the artists as "antennae". It asserts the superior diagnostic power of the poet over philosopher and "theorist" and, thereby, among other things, challenges Plato's triumphant preference some ten years before Derrida's *De la Grammatologie* began to perform the same service. As always, the verse promotes the primacy of declaration, parataxis and repetitive rhythm over any "explanation",[10] with its machinery of abstracted syntax. In this, the poem is cautionary for the theory-polluted and (now) over-institutionalised argument about postmodernism itself – and on the crucial plane of human language. Ginsberg implicitly proposes that the only point outside the ideological web, and the only fitting language, is the *prophetic*. All other perception and language are implicated in postmodern illusion:

> Machinery of a mass electrical dream! A war-creating Whore of Babylon bellowing over Capitols and *Academies!*
> (170; my emphasis)

The slightly later and longer poem "Television Was a Baby Crawling Toward That Deathchamber" was organised around the electrocution of the Rosenbergs as (Russian) communist spies – the event itself displays the shadow side of the "electric age". Here television replaces radio as the central postmodern index. If backgrounded by "the Marxist gramophone" (playing Mozart, no less), the lines maximise a quasi-televisual, heterogeneous

interconnectivity which serves as a radar spread of the contemporary sphere. The filmic image is exploited, but with intelligent ironic distantiation: "the Peacock spreads its cosmic-eye
Magnificat-feathered tail over its forgotten Ass" (273). This is
Incarnational associationism, linking the "cosmic-eye" pretension
of television networking to an Eliotic realm of "dung and death".
At the same time, the poem connects privately-controlled systems
of mass communication to the psychosomatic fantasies of some
"invisible six-headed billionaire" in terms of rapistic informational
imperialism: "the penis of billionaires depositing professional
semen in my ear". Textuality (the *Journal American*), radio and
television are here conjoined in a hyperreality constructed out of
wealth and power.

Ginsberg is a comically "serious" witness:

> Six thousand movietheatres, 100,000,000 television sets, a billion
> radios, wires and wireless criss crossing hemispheres … .
>
> (280)

The poet was alert to the decentred (yet still manipulated) power of
mass communication at an early stage in its hegemonic rise. He was
also insistently aware (despite the "Betty Boop" self-caricature) that
political power and informational rhetoric come mutually intertwined: "Hallooo I am coming end of my Presidency… – landslide
for Reader's Digest" (279). The poem was drafted on methedrine
(Ginsberg had also experimented with marijuana, ayahuasca,
psilocybin and LSD), yet between either hallucinogenics or
meditation Ginsberg's finished poetry was always controlled by an
inclusive but also selective intelligence. For instance, there is a brief
but highly tactical use of the typographical headlines pioneered in
Wyndham Lewis's *BLAST*: "ASSASSINATE!/ INVADE! STARVE
OUT! …". "Kulchur 61" is articulated as the sphere of "America",
unimpressed by some "old frog-looking editor worried about his
Aesthetics". This is ultimately justified because the poem confronts
both the symbolic and actual springs of current international power:

> Screech out over the radio that Standard Oil is … in the whole
> universe like an egotistical cancer.
>
> (275)

In the face of this the poet insists (like the Beatles' later Walrus?) that "I am the One, you are the One, we are the One". So "Life is waving, the cosmos is sending a message to itself". The final message is the need for spiritual liberation from postmodern technocracy: "O Widen the Area of Consciousness! O". Blake is once again evoked against the perpetual materialistic revolution unleashed in the seventeenth century by such as John Locke.

"Wichita Vortex Sutra" (1966) is a kind of versified *On the Road*. Though it is, in many ways, typical of the kind of poetry we associate with Ginsberg, its mode of composition contributed to a more collagistic effect. As the poet travelled to Kansas in his Volkswagen bus (driven by his friend Peter Orlovsky), he recorded his impressions of the countryside and the Vietnam War-fraught radio broadcasts he heard into a portable reel-to-reel Uher tape machine bought for him by the generosity of Bob Dylan.[11] Then he edited it, as always, for the page and fashioned it into a Neal Cassady style Odyssey of motoring adventure into "electric age" America, which culminates in a prophetic unmaking of the War: "The war is over now – "(411). It is dated 14 February 1966.

Ginsberg himself described the poem as "Shelleyan". However, his years of training in market research gave him a sense of just how the Vietnam War might offend the moral conscience of the greater USA (not in John Birch country) and the poem was able to make a political contribution in a way Shelley's poems (the most radical of which were witheld from publication in his lifetime) could not and did not – for all the myth. At the same time, the aesthetics of the verse range far beyond nineteenth century Romanticism. The word "Vortex", central to the title and reinvoked in the body of the poem, connects it up with *BLAST* 1914 and the original programme of Wyndham Lewis and Ezra Pound to assert a New Age: "O man of America, be born!" intones the poet in Whitmanesque vein. But the concrete anchoring of the rhetoric is in incisive epiphanies reminiscent of Pound's Imagism and Lewis's stylistic *coups* in *Enemy of the Stars*:[12]

> Red sun setting flat plains west streaked with gauzy veils,
>   chimney mist spread
> around christmas-tree-bulbed refineries – aluminum ...
>
>   (394)

The pastoral and the "postindustrial" commingle in a quasi-filmic verbal texture constantly broken up by electronic–oral interruptions: "'Bad Guess?' chorused the Reporters" (398).

The theme of "language, language" is an insistent one in this seventeen-page sequence. Towards the end the poet intrudes his own "search" for "the right language" into the content, as he also allows the radiovoice of Dylan to prepare the beginning of an ending. For "hyperlanguage" of every kind – headlines, billboard slogans, official statistics, radio catches, etc. – is registered and exposed in the poem as deadly linguistic inflation and pollution. As the ideogrammic method of Pound's *Cantos* lies behind the poetic style, so Pound's redaction "The Chinese Written Character as a Medium for Poetry" is evoked (400–1): yet Ginsberg knows that language is a "war" just as "the war is language" and the older poet's dream of a language of integral presence and maximum expressivity is used as a signpost not a solution. For "Advertisement" – a rhetorical zone where business, government and the military interconnect – is what Ginsberg's extended travelogue/diatribe attempts to undo by rhythm, image and invocation. The intent (bolstered by the presence of selected gurus) is to turn the "American language" into a "mantra".

The poem is divided into two parts – the first (interestingly) dated the day *after* the second. This first (and considerably shorter) section operates as a kind of prelude, scene-setting as much in terms of expectational fantasy as imagistic detail. A quasi-Islamic religious excitement modulates into self-assertion ("I am I") – perverse ecstasy of the speedeffect spliced with the sense of adventure – which strangely reverses into a chimera of self-destruction ("Pouf!") and settles, lamenting, at "Zero Street". The second section elaborates the world of the "Pepsi Generation", organised around the controlling margin of the Wichita "vortex", which is itself connected through the contemporary media to Vietnam and US military and political power world-wide. The evidence of mounting American commitment to the war and increasing casualties on both sides is chronicled at a specific and important moment of escalation (Ginsberg's documentary thoroughness[13] is as impressive as his bardic self-projection) and this, in turn, is relayed outwards in terms of feedback in Saigon, Peking, Moscow – and, indeed, the "youth of Liverpool". The White House consultative estimation of Viet Cong casualties per month, 3500, is used as a leitmotif which is combined with terse political sound bites justifying national intentions to fearful local youths who will be required as drafted personnel. The poet announces the end of the war – much as a later demonstration would wishfully attempt to elevate the Pentagon through communal meditation. He also invokes his mother's terror of anti-communist persecution. But his last thought is for the children in the area – the newest generation: arguably, though the struggle was long, it was this sentiment which would prove decisive in the ending of the war.

Ginsberg's stance in the poem is as an "old man now". In fact, he was only forty – and at the height of·his powers. But what is remarkable is that a poet who originally made his reputation in the jazz-and-consumerism mid-fifties was able not only to identify with, but to textually articulate, the pop rebelliousness of the next decade – to find, indeed, "the right language". Actually, his "antennae" and prophetic mode of expression remained effective into the seventies Punk era and beyond and his career well accommodated the coming together of verse and music, which eventually had him (quite remarkably) singing Blake's "Nurse's song", to guitar and hand-organ, on British television in the eighties.[14] His "Prophecy" retained its receptive (and dialogical) sense of what "America" was about in unfolding postmodernity – where its dynamic might be malign and which tone, directed to which audience (mainly the young, uncommitted to institutions and electronically rocking) – was most tellingly appropriate. His self-image has been, of course, a committed "(de-)construction". He dissolves himself to become a medium expressing "Future speeding on swift wheels".

The poet's "America", here, is a vortex where power, with all its international dimensions, comes infiltrated at local small-town level but is magnified everywhere by hyperreal media messages. This contrasts quite strongly to Jean Baudrillard's *Amérique* of exactly thirty years later, where the zone is "Utopia" as "desert". Despite the time gap, this may mainly be the difference between an insider and outsider view. Ginsberg's journey is that of the American beat prophet; Baudrillard's incursion (an almost parodic return of *On the Road* mythology) is that of the European, intellectual tourist. In ways, one feels Baudrillard understands as little about "America" as Julia Kristeva (earlier) about "Chinese Women". Yet I suspect there is a deeper difference here: Baudrillard (fresh from his meditations on the Beaubourg) *sees*, Ginsberg (friend of the pop

lyricists) above all *hears*. It is much like the difference between
Wyndham Lewis and James Joyce in the twenties – the "space
man" versus the "time man"[15] or, put differently, eye versus ear.
Although he has been accused of being an anti-modern postmodernist,[16] Baudrillard's position can be represented as against
both modernism and postmodernism, defined in a certain way. It is
suggestively similar to Lewis's (similarly "Nietzschean") scorn for
that "time philosophy" which links both modernism and postmodernism (though this is rarely noted today), as expressed, for
instance, in *Time and Western Man* (1927) and *The Childermass* (1928).
The latter book, most particularly, evokes a hyperreal "desert" in
some science fiction (afterlife) zone which interconnects both urban
and pastoral constructions of complete artificiality. This scenario
too "evokes", as Baudrillard says of his "America", "the end of the
world". Both Lewis and Baudrillard, one might say, are essentially
Western rationalists excoriating the dissipation of rationalism into
fluxive simulacra.

Ginsberg, however, is not a rationalist but a Blakean visionary. He both celebrates and denounces the hyperreality of
"America", depending on its effects – not for some dream of a fixed
neo-Platonic ordering of Forms, but in terms of human suffering or
fulfilment. He is Tiresias not Oedipus, Isaiah not Aristotle, poet not
philosopher, visionary not theorist. Hence, the poem is a
mythologisation and prophecy not an "analysis" and it celebrates
life as well as it denounces death dealing. "America", here, is
neither Utopia nor desert but a vortex of signs (and wonders)
rooted in local peculiarities as well as cosmic human desires and
fears – pitched somewhere between devastation and "millennium".
The intensity of ambivalence in "Wichita Vortex Sutra" remains
persuasive in the context of the self-implosion of the Cold War, the
rise of ecological apocalypticism – and with spare years before the
double millennium. It effects an irregularly rhythmic, collagistic
postmodern language as a language of insight and liberation to
confront the information fall-out of postmodernity. And it asserts
(democratically) that this poetic language "is also yours" (406).

"Birdbrain!" (1980) takes Ginsberg's artistic career into the
America of Ronald Reagan. However, although "earthed" in the
Pentagon and CIA ("Fatass Bucks!"), "America" here has become
international postmodernity itself: for example, "Russia Yugoslavia
England Poland Argentina United States El Salvador/ ... China".
Perhaps influenced by Ted Hughes' metamorphic postmodern

harlequin "Crow" (see below, Chapter 6), "Birdbrain!" denominates human "Will to Truth" as diminutive, caricatural power fantasy in action.

At the same time, "I am birdbrain!" The poem culminates in its own writing act – as a bid for "immortality". Hence, "Birdbrain!" stands for the human project in general – including the poet's own inevitable implication in it. The central character is a kind of Merry Prankster with the worst motivations of a Hell's Angel.[17] Birdbrain pollutes, destroys, creates wars, pens propaganda, commits genocide and threatens the entire planet. The figure is specifically masculinist, refraining from sexuality so that "his dong will grow big that way" (739). As in Hughes' *Crow*, comedy and horror come bizarrely interfused, with the poet a portentous clown in the centre, who declares that Birdbrain has won the International Poetry Contest. But the poetry does not matter – the poetry is in the fantastic and hortatory vision.

Nevertheless, the verse is more cunningly contrived than a quick glance through the lines might suggest. This is easily accessible poetry for anyone with basic literacy – hence, there is a familiar refusal of modernist élitism. Yet the very loosely rhythmic and simplistically paratactical mode establishes itself on the page (or in the ear) as a specially forged postmodernist pop-art speech. Each line (with very occasional variations) conforms to a minimalist grammatical pattern: subject – verb – object phrases/clauses. So a kind of hypnotic verbal format is set up – rather like the sound units of Terry Riley's music or a mixer's automatic riff:

> Birdbrain ran FBI 30 years appointed by F. D. Roosevelt and
> never chased Cosa Nostra! ...
>
> (738)

The technique establishes a primary grammatical code (with mutations as well as variations) which replicates the basic characteristics of information technology. The pattern is more important than any specific message in any line – and indeed many of the images could be completely altered without really effecting the meaning of the whole. "Birdbrain" is the first-word subject of all but five lines in this fifty-eight-line poem. The effect (somewhat like a Beckett play) is to reduce the whole human project to a robotic stammering – generated, ultimately, by dangerous fantasies and acts of lethal banality.

Legend has tended to fix Ginsberg's verse in the "underground" of the fifties and sixties. This may be partly his own fault (he was overprone to attribute both genius and sainthood to friends of his "Beatnik" beginnings), but the myth is diminishing to his contribution overall. For at least forty years, Ginsberg was in the front row of the postmodern spectacular, reporting (and translating) with precision, humour, moral probity and passion. While American poetic discrimination overvalued the New Critical qualities of early Robert Lowell and British poetasters inflated the neo-Georgian preciosities of Philip Larkin, Ginsberg's verse registered both the melodrama and nuances of the "electric age" long before postmodernity was given a name or embarrassed by a theorisation. Ginsberg's "America", as attested throughout *Collected Poems*, was a valid figuration of what was actually going on – in terms readily available to anyone with ears to hear.

From the standpoint of the nineties, the Ginsberg persona is less important for its aura of "The Beat Generation" than for its embodiment of what is now discussed as postmodernism. There are a number of relevant qualities. Ginsberg was steeped in modernism as in the Romantics; but by *Howl*, at least, he had decisively broken with both formal metrics and High Culture anti-formality. He chose psalmic parataxis and hypnotic linear repetition to make the "poetic" available to the public at large. His work is, in a sense, "depthless" and also non-"serious", but it by no means lacks moral sincerity or incisiveness of critique (and his personal challenges to established power have been legion). At the same time, humour, play and self-parody co-exist with anger, mockery and outrage. His work was *in* the world of multinational finance and super-advertisement yet not *of* it: both wit and an ultimately religious vision made his writing parasitically enervating of the malign world body he inhabited and gave his readers a holographic breakdown of where they, themseves, were living. In his work, historical quotationality is both overt (Buddha, Islam, the Kaddish) and interwoven in the texture of free verse itself – the prophets, the *Sutras*, Blake, Whitman, Pound. Yet there is a strong contemporaneity and Ginsbergian authenticity to everything he has written. The lengthened shadow of Ginsberg becomes a foreshadowing of postmodernism itself.

In many ways his contribution is in contrast to that of Auden (though Auden apparently appreciated his work):[18] the British-born poet recycled traditional subtleties of versification, whereas the American "bard" pioneered "open field", expansive free verse, even looser, bolder and more demotic than the experimentation of Pound and Williams. Nevertheless, both Auden and Ginsberg spoke back to the developing tropes of electronic communication – the former by deft aphorism (as opposed to slogan), the latter by appropriating the repetitive, agglutinative style of media programming. It is likely that "Howl" and "Kaddish" will maintain their reputations for somewhat different qualities – and that is appropriate. But Ginsberg's particular significance for postmodern poetry, in general, lies in his work's prophetic registration of unprecedented experience ("my generation"), its development of verbal and linear freedom through fluency and its unique combination of self-deprecating comic buffoonery and radically-engaged personal and political passion. Allen Ginsberg's poetry still constitutes a comedic *conscience*[19] for the postmodern world.

Notes

1. Allen Ginsberg, *Collected Poems 1947–1980* (Penguin, 1984). All quotations are from this edition.
2. See Francis Fukuyama, *The End of History and the Last Man* (The Free Press, 1992).
3. Courageously published by the City Lights Bookshop, San Francisco in 1956 – in defiance of the uptight orthodoxies of the New Criticism.
4. James Joyce, *A Portrait of the Artist as a Young Man*, first published in *Egoist* (1915).
5. I think the jargon is justified in this case. See Louis Althusser, *Politics and History* (New Left Books, 1972) and *For Marx* (New Left Books, 1977).
6. Here again theory becomes genuinely explanatory. See McLuhan, *The Gutenberg Galaxy*; Walter J. Ong, *Orality and Literacy: The Technologizing of the Word* (Methuen, 1982); and Elizabeth L. Eisenstein, *The Printing Revolution in Early Modern Europe* (Cambridge University Press, 1983).
7. American and British radicals seem to have rather different attitudes to the word "serious". Antony Easthope in his *British Poststructuralism Since 1968* (Routledge, 1991), p. 172, records a revealing exchange between himself ("questioner") and Richard Rand at the 1981 "Text" conference at Southampton University. I recall the confrontation in somewhat terser terms:

EASTHOPE (*aggressively*): Will you *ever* be serious?
RAND (*Bob Hope jaw and wagging finger*): Oh-er ... I regard seriousness as a ... major form of repression.

8. That is, to tell the present as it is, as well as foretell the future.
9. A phrase much bandied about in the Britain of the eighties by admirers of such as Keith Joseph and Margaret Thatcher. One learnt at school that "matter can neither be created nor destroyed": nor can wealth; it is merely a redistribution of resources ultimately dependent on (finite) nature. Adam Smith enquired into the "Wealth of Nations" – not its "creation".
10. "Explanation means *ex plane*, that is to say, the opening out of things on a plain surface ... the intellect distorts reality ... because it persists in unfolding things out in space" (T. E. Hulme, *Speculations: Essays on Humanism and the Philosophy of Art*, ed. Herbert Read (Routledge & Kegan Paul, 1965 [originally published 1924]), pp. 381–5).
11. See Barry Miles, *Ginsberg: A Biography* (Penguin, 1990), pp. 381–5.
12. See *BLAST 1* (reissued by Black Sparrow Press, 1981), pp. 59–85 and my account of Lewis's style in Dennis Brown, *Intertextual Dynamics within the Literary Group – Joyce, Lewis, Pound and Eliot: The Men of 1914* (Macmillan, 1990), pp. 60–4.
13. For details of his research file see Miles, *Ginsberg*, pp. 435–6.
14. "Writers in Conversation", *Allen Ginsberg with R. D. Laing* (ICA Video, 1985).
15. See my *Intertextual Dynamics*, pp. 95–7, 111–15, 127–30.
16. See Mike Gane, *Baudrillard: Critical and Fatal Theory* (Routledge, 1991), pp. 178–82.
17. Ginsberg, of course, was present at the uneasy meeting of both groups. See Miles, *Ginsberg*, pp. 377–9.
18. See *ibid.*, p. 231.
19. I mean this in its Anglo-Saxon (moral) sense: but in French "conscience" means "consciousness" (as in Henri Bergson's proto-modernist text *Essai sur les données immédiates de la conscience*, 1889), and this sense fits Ginsberg's contribution too. I have often wondered whether James Joyce had the French, as much as the English, sense of the word in mind when on the last page of *Portrait of the Artist* Stephen vows to "forge ... the uncreated conscience of my race".

4

Sylvia Plath's "Ariel"

Sylvia Plath's posthumous collection *Ariel*[1] was published in 1965 and rapidly transformed her life and life's work into a legend which remains compelling, controversial[2] and proleptically contemporaneous. She is postmodern in still being very much "one of us":[3] her work, as Jacqueline Rose's recent title puts it, constitutes a "haunting" – and what haunts *us* most tellingly is the degree to which her domestic[4]-confessional, mature style operates as a kind of personalised fuse-box (the brilliance of those terminal flashings) for the highly charged tensions criss-crossing the interconnected networks of the "electric age". As a particular style – the compressed, psychic scenarios, *ostinato* rhythms and precise, hectic images – her writing registers postmodernity as a site of decentred and fragmented selfhood where, nevertheless, the ontological fractures of the linguistic "subject" coincide with the fraught inescapability of agency (an experiential reality recently re-emphasised in the wake of poststructuralist scepticism).[5] "To be, or not to be" in a mutating contemporary era .... and if so, what: mother, abandoned wife, harpy, man-eater, suicide, Electra or golden poet as Ariel? The selfhood wherein such tensions are played out comes earthed in crustacean sensitivity (the open–shut "seashell") yet is also the self electric – a matter of "filaments", "wires", "short circuits", "lanterns" (obsessed with telephones) and flickering dangerously "off,on,off,on". The poems rehearse, with self-conscious fictive art, the possibilities of the split agent in the world after Hitler and Hiroshima, as felt in one young life. And the last choice of being – end game – preoccupied both the words and the woman: to "put out the light, and then put out the light".

"Ariel" represents the option of positive creativity – or, put another way, the brilliant manufacture of a personalised psycho-social hyperreality, rooted always in the "blood-jet" and bone, the chores of a varied domesticity and the terrors and flying ecstasies of the wrestling human soul. In one particular poem of her "Juvenilia" ("Aerialist", 331–2), Plath lays down some of the chief aspects of Ariel's role – the "dream" dimension, "acrobatics" ("gilded") in a "gigantic hall" where the protagonist gains "applause" as "outrageous nimble queen" (with nine lives), leaping through some imaginative "hoop" – only to wake to the alarm clock and the mundane "steel gauntlets" of postmodern "traffic". The circus itself is strictly contemporaneous, with its "tall trucks" and so akin to the general street hustle, but "her act" is of the air, airy and so both of and a projection beyond the "electric age" *banale*. "The Hanging Man" (1960, 141–2) gives placement to the alternative Shakespearean scenario ("pinned ... in this tree"). Plath knew Auden's idea of Ariel[6] and in the first two lines of this short poem, gives it vivid rearticulation:

> By the roots of my hair some god got hold of me.
> I sizzled in his blue volts like a desert prophet.

Yet her choice here seems to be for imprisonment itself against the "boredom" of "bald white days in a shadeless socket". Nevertheless, the ambition of pitting imaginative invention against "global village" simulacra remained. The poem "Ariel" (1962, 239–40) rewrites an earlier horse-riding poem ("Whiteness I remember", 1958, 102–3) to make "Almost thrown, not / Thrown" into an Expressionist and Minimalist lyrical gem.

The emotive energy in the poem "Ariel" is about as "valent"[7] as textuality could make it: the poem represents the humming flight of an impassioned arrow. The first line invokes a dark stillness in three concise words (realistically, perhaps, the stables – dramatically the static instant before lift-off). "Then ...": after this word the "Aerialist" is free of both trapeze and maestro, an angelic[8] free agent, flying yet self-directed. But she is also peculiarly impelled: "Hauls me ... / I unpeel ... / ... foam / ... am the arrow"!. Neither the horse, Ariel, nor Plath's actual body are much to the point here: though expressed through crisp physical images, the poem asserts a spiritual transcendence beyond mere being. Plath has constructed an "Ariel" as pure imaginative project out of the "substanceless blue" to direct one pole of her poetry toward a vision of "morning". Yet, tragically, even this flight is qualified as "suicidal". The manic self-projection includes its own flip-side depression, anticipating the roller-coaster imaginative mood swing of so much of the best electronic pop lyricism. And if Émile Durkheim was right in reading suicide itself as ultimately a social manifestation then this, as other of Plath's poems, serves as "defense early warning system" of a postmodern ecstasy-in-hyperreality always betrayed by all-too incarnate "Death Instinct".[9]

"Fever 103° " helps indicate quite why this might be so:

Radiation turned it white
And killed it in an hour.

(231)

A high temperature is here the "objective correlative" for a key postmodern trauma – personal, political and international. The poem swings between such a hell and possible Paradise through (again) dazzling accumulation of contemporary imagery and "quotational" allusion, always recognisably anchored in the fever state: as R. D. Laing (approximately) once put it, we are all within some five degrees Fahrenheit of effective psychosis. In fact, it is a general modern literary perception to construe "selves" as "dissolving".[10] What Plath importantly adds to this beyond the image *juste* (staple of (post)modern lyricists from Pound to Paul Simon) is a uniquely insistent rhythm, grounded in an abrasively iambic unit:

... the sin, the sin.
... off,on,off,on.
  Not him, not him ....

The poem exercises a personal "I" which is also culturally exemplary, linking Cerberus to Isadora Duncan, Botany to Hiroshima, Christian typology to Japanese craftmanship. Not uncommonly in the 1962 poems, "Fever 103°" ends in rising assertion – already a prime symbolic *motif* for hubristic postmodernity (the rocket-launch). The mother of two children becomes here transmogrified into a "pure acetylene / Virgin", "going up" on the "rise" – Ariel ascending.

"Daddy" is also primarily a triumph of pure fictionality. Of course, it is rooted in psychic realities – but which ones exactly?[11] Just as "Electra on Azalea Path" (1959, 116–7) subsumes a psychoanalytic "complex" into a knowing fictional pose (and this raises the question of quite how a self-advertised condition can still be said to be of the *Un*conscious) so here the verse is exhibitionistic rather than unknowing of its deep psychic structure and surface literariness alike. Traumatic pain is exercised and to a degree exorcised through flamboyant fictive artifice employing a range of literary devices – urgent nursery-rhyme rhythm, the Exodus myth of liberation, the anti-vampire ritual killing and the deployment of almost comic book clichés of Nazism, sometimes self-contradictory in its vehement demonisation (panzer and Luftwaffe in the one villain!). As Jacqueline Rose has pointed out (and with reference to psychoanalytic studies of actual Holocaust victim behaviour), Plath is also able to switch uneasily between victim and oppressor positions – and there remains that weirdly troubling line: "Every woman adores a Fascist" .... The poet's own reading suggestions for "Daddy" would make it into a kind of Expressionistic dramatic monologue – the protagonist an actual Jewish girl and the father (the imagined listener) a real Nazi. (In seminars I have found students reading the poem this "literally" without even the benefit of Plath's gloss: I imagine this is not atypical.) Altogether, whether one finds Plath's comments helpful or merely evasive, "Daddy" is far from being purely "Confessional". It is a highly wrought imaginative construction.

At the same time, it is clear that however provocatively appropriated here, Holocaust mythology cannot be regarded as mere Plathean fantasy. On the contrary, it has become an enduring nightmare for postmodern consciousness: as the German theologian Jürgen Moltmann has put it, "human self-confidence itself was lost in the abominations of Auschwitz .... 'man is dead' became the expression of twentieth century nihilism".[12] Such commonly hailed "postmodernist" novels as *Gravity's Rainbow* or *The White Hotel* are obsessed by Nazi atrocities; Plath's poem merely precedes them and is thus prophetic of that "historiographic metafiction" which far from constituting an epistemological game represents a drastic shake-up of "rational" history" to try to account for – or at least articulate – the horrors of a perverted modernity. And this helps explain the extremities of reader response to this poem – from awesome "recognition" to indignant outrage. Holocaust atrocity remains a nightmare haunting the brains of the living (as I write this chapter, something called "ethnic cleansing" is taking place in Bosnia–Herzogovina, the flashpoint for the first World War).

One biographical factor (which I have not seen enlarged on elsewhere) may help point up the ultimately geopolitical relevance of Plath's "personal" poem. The verse claims,"I was ten when they buried you". Sylvia was, of course, only just eight when her actual father died. "Ten" is, no doubt, a round "poetic" number; yet something traumatically important did happen when the poet was about ten years old – Germany/Austria, cultural root of both her parents, declared war on America in the aftermath of Pearl Harbour. Paul Johnson in his *History of the Modern World*, has described the reaction to this in the USA:

> America ... found itself instantly united, angry and committed to wage total war with all its outraged strength. Hitler's reckless declaration ... drew a full measure of this enormous fury down upon his own nation.[13]

The "man in black with a Meinkampf look" had effected a major fracture (only to be resolved by Unconditional Surrender) between Sylvia Plath's parental heritage of *Kultur* and the "All American" values (to include a liberal commitment to Civil Rights for all) with which she identified herself as a continuously brilliant student. The ultimate parental betrayal here concerns poisoned origins ("your root"). So the melodramatic fictionality concerns both the German language ("Ich, ich, ich, ich") and perverted Germanicity ("not very pure or true"). By the end, the Fascistic "Daddy" must himself become victimised in a fantasy of folk ritual revenge (one remembers Dresden – with Kurt Vonnegut). The poem attempts to exorcise the fatal corruption of a culture which underlay Plath's earliest identity and gave her a surname. It is this factor which gives some psychic validity to her making free with the imagery of the Holocaust – not a factor, presumably, which might apply to, say, D. M. Thomas.[14]

The brilliance of this poem – its rhythmic power, its dazzling development of shock imagery, its decisive (though ultimately ambiguous) *tour de force* of closure – have often been described. I wish only to make one further point about its contribution to the literature of postmodernity. Perhaps more than any other of Plath's poems, "Daddy" captures and enacts the "victim position" – that prized role in an anti-heroic era. While young Anglo/American men were still identifying themselves as Holden Caulfield or Jimmy Porter, the Angry Young Man or the White Negro, the Outsider or the Beat Saint (victim introjections all), Sylvia Plath provided younger Anglo/American women with an almost unbeatable riposte ("Barely daring to breathe or Achoo") – and laid down one kind of motivation for a counter-assertive Feminism. The plight of the oppressed, decentred and culture-warped individual has become the staple of postmodern cultural theory from Sartre to Cixous, Fanon to Foucault or Terry Eagleton to Toni Morrison. The ultimate villain is (of course) Power – whether capitalism, colonialism, masculinism or scientism. The "victim position" in this familiar structuration is the put-upon "heroine" and her fight-back (or tragic capitulation) remains a key motif in fiction making from Lesbian poetics to the Postcolonial novel. No doubt there is still much "Gutenberg" Hegel, Marx and Nietzsche informing this victimisation narrative (and it is vulnerable to "electric age" dialogism – as challenged, say, on the amazing Oprah Winfrey Show), yet postmodern cultural politics cannot so far do without it. "Daddy" is its *opus classicum* in the poetry of postmodernity and the fictive subtleties and contradictions the poem expresses so cannily remain of importance to the whole discussion about Power, the agent's options and, indeed, the problem of Evil.

"Lady Lazarus" again raises psychoanalytic/biographical questions which cannot be entirely evaded (for all that they have been quite thoroughly discussed elsewhere). In his book *Doubles*, Karl Miller has a lively and intelligent chapter entitled "Who is Sylvia?"[15] However, he scarcely attempts to answer his own question. As I suggested in a review of the book:

> the Professor seems to resort to the skills of the Edinburgh fencing school: "Every life is made up, put on, imagined – including, hypocrite lecteur, *yours*" (p. 348). Touché – yet this is surely a dusty answer for those who seek to sift truth from phantasy in the dark corners of the suffering mind.[16]

Plath (whichever "Sylvia") rehearsed and enacted suicide bids in both her art and her life – and in both, as it were, she succeeded. Suicide remains one option for agency in the era of postmodernity; at the same time, in Durkheim's terms, suicide may also be seen as a social symptom. Here the question becomes less "Who is Sylvia?" (or "Did she mean the last attempt to succeed?")[17] than "What in the post Second World War situation might cause so talented and intelligent a writer to even play with the idea?" And such a question must also come linked with an issue I seek to address more with respect to John Berryman – what caused so *many* postmodern American poets (at the very moment of America's world-ascendancy) to succumb to alcohol, drugs, psychiatric hospitalisation and frequently suicide itself? Why should early postmodernity produce a poetry of Death Instinct?

As in "Daddy", the Holocaust is a key source of imagery in "Lady Lazarus". However, in place of the "Aryan eye" emerges the demotic postmodern "peanut-crunching crowd" with its "same brute / Amused shout". So "Herr Doktor" refers not only to Nazi medical criminals but also to the all-licensed Health experts of a materialistic postmodernity. In both cases, it seems to be implied, the effective bottom-line is *worth*, in terms not of human dignity but economic viability. So soap, wedding ring and gold filling refer not only to the depraved financial reductionism of the Nazi regime but also, surely, to the increasing globalisation of monetary values where a "smiling woman" is only of account in ultimately fiscal terms. So for Plath (whose evoked American hospitalisations had to be financed by her hard-working mother), there is a "very large charge" for any relic of the "miracle" of her resurrection. In her final apotheosis she will "eat men", because contemporaneous value terms are implicitly written as masculinist at the expense of womanly living – for which a "big strip tease" must be provided as the price of being. So dying is an "art" this woman cultivates (the irony here is disconcertingly wayward and a "postmodernist" appropriation of street-wise phrases – "like hell", "feels real" – is apparent), leading to an inevitably "theatrical" return to life. That life is caught up in the "trash" priorities of the postmodern *banale* where she must function as "the same, identical woman" – until the next time. Perversely, the final act to which these lines look can itself be seen in "trash" terms as a kind of desperate literary "investment" which rocketed such poetry to almost instant acclaim. For which reason a poem like "Lady Lazarus" raises an unpleasant question in the mind – would it retain validity if the poet was still alive and well, perhaps with the Queen's Medal for poetry mounted above her hearth?

"Years" raises no such queries and adds a religious dimension which anticipates the mature work of R. S. Thomas but is rarely highlighted in critical accounts of her poetry. Though written in November, the poem apostrophises the Christmas season and questions its meaning. God's "vacuous black" stuck over with "confetti" stars is rejected; in its place is celebrated the motion of pistons and horses' hooves – "Ariel" as becoming, as speed and even as Yeatsian eschatology. At which point the phenomenon of "Christus" is interrogated via Eliot and (behind him) Blake – "a tiger this year ...?" Christ's desire to "fly" is contrasted with Nobodaddy's "stasis", thereby driving a horse and carriage through the dynamic God–Word–Son creational evolution announced in the prolegomena of St John's Gospel. Nevertheless, the reference to Christ ends in a question and the verse moves on to the stillness of evoked holly berries. At the conclusion, hooves and pistons prevail in mooted intimation of futuristic hyperactivity. What the poem seems to sponsor is a characteristically modern/postmodern sense of historically-accelerating motion, the mutual involvement of nature ("hooves") and culture ("pistons") in this and the undertow of an apocalyptic sense of ending ("be done with it"). Despite the deft disavowals and dangling queries, "Years", a most striking poem, reminds us that the condition of postmodernity represents, in however dissipated or debased a form, the latest manifestation of a Jewish–Christian culture out of which Western science, economics and geopolitics emerged and in which, I would argue, they are still implicated. But is the presiding Power now "Christus" or "Herr Lucifer"?

"Brasilia" queries this issue in terms of a projected "super-people" characterised as technological androids. The city of Brasilia remains perhaps the highest point of the architecture (and social engineering) of modernity – not the house, but the designed city, as a machine for living in. Plath contrasts it and its fantastic inhabitants to her unique, greasy and teething baby – untamed nature *soi-même*. And the child conjures up recollection of "the star, / The old story": mother earth is invoked as diurnal experience in the Devon countryside. Blake's Nobodaddy here consumes humankind "like light rays" – a touch of science fiction fantasia? Yet the foil here is surely T. S. Eliot who in *Four Quartets* conflated the Christian "dove" into the reality of German bombers over London,[18] as Dantesque reminder that we are consumed "by either fire or fire". Plath prays that her child may be unredeemed by such "annihilation" (seen here as logocentric "power" and "glory"). It is an odd conclusion – for bland "super-people" are precisely what a purely secular modernity was likely to promote (the "orange lollies on silver sticks" of "The Munich Mannequins", 161–3). For Eliot such "Brasilians" could only be "hollow men". Yet Plath seems to prefer hollowness to redemptive pain for her child; she prays for his preservation as "mirror" – it is understandable, but mirror of what if not incipient Brasilia?

"Mystic" (268–9) is another poem of religious questioning and meditation. The questions, we are told, are "without answers", but the poem goes on to avow that "Meaning leaks from the molecules". Dated just ten days before her death, the lines evoke memories of forest summers and sailing ships out of a domestic situation set amongst city chimneys. The dramatic key question is placed in the second section: "Once one has seen God, what is the remedy?" The usual versions of Plath's work and life do not easily prepare us to know what to make of such a line – no in-turned anger, no revenge scenarios, no man-baiting and no witchy self-mythologisation. Even more than "Years", "Mystic" addresses the situation of the contemporary in terms of that taboo joker in the cultural pack – teleology. And here the sense of purpose includes an experience of Divinity. Again Christ is invoked, as is Christianity itself ("the Communion tablet"), but the verse questions whether the sea bears any memory of one said to have walked on it. In doubts of a "great love" the poem affirms tenderness – and moves toward a kind of benediction for the children in their cots, the sunshine and the still-beating heart. It is a more relaxed piece than we are used to associate with Plath – the rhythm almost conversational, the sentences leisurely rather than dramatically abrupt and an initial show of surprise imagery dissolving into an accumulation of humble metonymic details, such as the "humpback in his small, washed cottage".

The most dramatic (and self-dramatising) part of the poem occurs when Plath evokes the seizure and using of the "subject" by divine power. Thereafter, the lines move meditatively to their conclusion in almost upbeat acceptance. Neither this poem nor "Years" was included in Plath's selection for *Ariel*, presumably because they were written too late, but one wonders if she would have included them anyway, for they scarcely fit into the self-mythologisation characteristic of the collection. Their pared-down directness contrasts sharply, for instance, with the cluttered imagery and allusive portentousness of the "Bee" poems. And "Mystic", in particular, suggests that postmodernity cannot be solely represented in terms of Holocaust-horror on the one hand, psychic trauma on the other. The poem implicitly queries how the "global village", with all its energised children, ever came to crystallise out in historical time from the primal chemistry soup of the Big Bang – and why.

"Edge" is the last poem in the Hughes *Collection* and is dated "5 February 1963" (Plath died on the 11th). It is about a dead woman with her dead children (Plath however sealed her own children's room before turning on the gas) and has been inevitably read as a personal farewell. This remains valid: in the light of "Mystic", however, one can also read the poem in far more global terms. "Mystic" ponders the meaning of city domesticity in a universe of interpretative "molecules" and the "mill" of questions thus generated: "Edge", we might say, contemplates the extinction of natural life on earth as seen from a planetary perspective (the moon). The woman herself is likened to a rose which closes when "the garden stiffens". If "personally" she is Sylvia Plath herself, then universally she is Gaia or Mother Nature. Classical "necessity" is evoked to explain a sense of accomplishment: "We have come so far, it is over". Hence, both nature and history are "perfected" – completed. Milk has dried up and night odours "bleed". If Plath might have imagined this scenario in the shadow of Hiroshima, thirty years on the poem speaks as much in terms of that chronic pollution and wastage of natural resources which has accompanied the global overproduction which feeds the stock exchange computers of postmodernity. Plath's last textual representation of earth is beamed back, as it were, from an already dead planet on which, six years ahead, human feet will walk. Its message is admonitory in its dour stoicism: "She is used to this sort of thing".

"Ariel" – as the perfected[19] poetic vision of postmodernity I have tried to describe – was the product of less than a year's work (May 1962–February 1963). Among other things, Plath's imaginative spirit succeeded in creating a powerful allegory of her own life and death which has remained exemplary (and cautionary), in its way, ever since. That allegorical zone of being constitutes, most especially, the feminine body and psyche as representative terrain where the postmodern realises itself as both memory and aspiration. In this realm both the electric chair[20] and electrotherapy combine to produce an Electra torn between parental legacy and the present needs of her children. This is not a merely private encoding. So, though superficially Plath can appear as an Eisenhower era superbrat (a kind of word-dazzling Marylin Monroe), her "Ariel" is obsessed by nationalistic arrogance, language alterity, territorial jockeying and ethnic hatred which looks both before and (prophetically) after the Cold War to address, also, a Europe which is "other" to, yet inextricably and increasingly implicated in, the American advent of the postmodern. And into this heady brew of national and cultural interpenetrations intrudes an impassioned (and personally jaundiced?) version of the gender war which remains explosive. The "Ariel" persona – so persuasive and so deceptively complex – rehearses options, fictionalises strategies and exercises a mythology of self-destruction and resurrection which ultimately put the writer in ultimate danger. Whatever the tragic outcome in biographical terms, that mythologisation remains – if somewhat premature from a nineties perspective – one possibility of self-placement within the postmodern condition.

In the meantime, "Ariel" is also a way of seeing the public sphere (which the self can introject in a number of ways) and provides a scenario in which to shape the response of agency. The imagery is perhaps most successful in representing this sphere and rebukes the coming banalities of the "camcorder" as it provides a precedent for the lyrics of the best electronic troubadours. The exact and exacting image ("the day outside glides by like ticker tape") becomes irrefutable (as advertisers know so well). In Plath's verse it comes combined with "quotational" allusiveness contracted to a telling metonymy:

> The Lioness,
> The shriek in the bath,
> The cloak of holes.
>
> ("Purdah", 244)

And both the imagery and allusions are everywhere animated by a nervous, characteristically repetitive rhythm ("But how about the eyes, the eyes, the eyes", 210), which links psychic intensity to the future iterative tropes of international CNN and MTV. The short lyric has been chosen (after Yeats, in defiance of *Four Quartets* and the Pisan Cantos) as the codeform of postmodern poetic articulation – Crazy Jane curtly allegorising in manic free verse. And the most striking lyrics, for all their honed excellence, have something of the populist fantasy structuring of the stories Plath constantly sent to such magazines as *Seventeen* or *Mademoiselle*.[21] The poems constitute an extraordinary and volatile mixture. Brilliant imagery, allusive resonance, remarkably insistent rhythm and rapid psychodrama scenarios – in this form "Ariel" lives on as dazzling text. In my opinion, such an enduring "Ariel" is worth far more attention than the debatable circumstances of Plath's failed marriage or premature death. For "Ariel" still expresses the complexities of all private/public human experience in the postmodern era and in a poem like "Mystic", at least, that vision remains to offer a meaning to live towards.

Notes

1. The Faber and Faber *Ariel* remains powerfully popular and has effected its own allegory of the Plath contribution; however, it is by no means identical with the *Ariel* which Plath had planned. I have used throughout the later Sylvia Plath, *Collected Poems*, ed. with an Introduction by Ted Hughes (Faber and Faber, 1981): here all the poems are given in chronological order of composition.
2. For instance, when Jacqueline Rose's book *The Haunting of Sylvia Plath* appeared (Virago, 1991) there was quite vigorous newspaper debate, including letters from Ted Hughes and the author. See also Anne Stevenson, *Bitter Fame: A Life of Sylvia Plath* (Penguin, 1990) and Ronald Hayman, *The Death and Life of Sylvia Plath* (Heinemann, 1991).
3. Marlow's phrase about Jim in Joseph Conrad, *Lord Jim* (Penguin, 1986), for example, p. 351.
4. Cf. "I have chosen this term, rather than M. L. Rosenthal's better-known 'confessional poem' because confessional poem implies a confession rather than a making .... I shall define the domestic poem as one that represents and comments on a protagonist's relationship to one or more family members, usually a parent, child, or spouse" (Steven Gould Axelrod, *Sylvia Plath: The Wound and the Cure of Words* (Johns Hopkins University Press, 1990), p. 59).
5. See, for instance, Anthony Giddens, *Social Theory and Modern Sociology* (Polity Press, 1990), *Modernity and Self-Identity* (Polity Press, 1991) and Zygmunt Bauman, *Intimations of Postmodernity* (Routledge, 1992). See, too, Anthony Elliott, "Finding One's Self in a Self-less World", *The Times Higher*, 10 July 1992: the books reviewed here are Jonathan Scott Lash and Jonathan Friedman (eds), *Modernity and Identity* (Blackwell, 1992), Anthony J. Cascardi, *The Subject of Modernity* (Cambridge University Press, 1992) and Seyla Benhabib, *Situating the Self: Gender, Community and Postmodernity in Contemporary Theory* (Polity Press, 1992). For a more literary view of issues concerning identity and agency see, for instance, Robert Langbaum, *The Mysteries of Identity: A Theme in Modern Literature* (University of Chicago Press, 1977), Karl Miller, *Doubles: Studies in Literary History* (Oxford University Press, 1985), Dennis Brown, *The Modernist Self in Twentieth-Century English Literature: A Study in Self-Fragmentation* (Macmillan, 1989) and Patrick Grant, *Literature and Personal Values* (Macmillan, 1992).

6. "W. H. Auden had once told her that 'Caliban is the natural bestial projection, Ariel the creative imagination' ... like the 'airy spirit' of Shakespeare's play, Plath wanted to transcend her rival, the 'man–animal'" (Axelrod, *Sylvia Plath*, p. 67). An important mentor of Plath's, Robert Lowell had the nickname "Cal", of course.

7. I have borrowed this term from group psychoanalysis to mean "extra-responsive to psychic intensity". See W. R. Bion, *Experiences in Groups and Other Papers* (Tavistock, 1972).

8. In *Paradise Lost* (6.371) John Milton makes "Ariel" one of the fallen angels. In H. D. 's "Tribute to the Angels" both "Uriel" and "Annael" are good angels: see *Trilogy* (Carcanet, 1988), p. 79.

9. Freud's revisionary theory was, of course, partly developed out of the Great War experience. See Ernest Jones, *The Life and Work of Sigmund Freud*, ed. and abridged by Lionel Trilling and Steven Marcus (Penguin, 1977), pp. 424–47. It would be interesting to know if Plath had read Norman O. Brown's 1959 book *Life Against Death*, which for all its liberational project tended to affirm a preponderance of Death Instinct in the current cultural scene. Sociologists have tended to interpret Durkheim's work thus: "while suicide seems to be a voluntary act, undertaken by an individual alone, in fact it expresses general properties of social causation". See Giddens, *Social Theory and Modern Sociology*, p. 190.

10. See my chapter "Dissolving Self", *The Modernist Self*, pp. 14–42.

11. I read a paper on "The Fictive Structuring of Demonisation: Sylvia Plath's 'Daddy'" to the "Psychoanalysis and the Public Sphere Conference", East London Polytechnic in November 1991. In discussion afterwards, at least two practising psychotherapists suggested that the deepest anger in the poem is, in fact, against "Mummy": the line cited to support this was: "Every woman adores a Fascist".

12. Jürgen Moltmann, *Theology Today* (Student Christian Movement Press, 1990), p. 87. Cf.: "For Lyotard, history – and Auschwitz is the case he always comes back to – is ... a succession of such experiences by 'silent', or better silenced minorities" (Lash and Friedman, *Modernity and Identity*, p. 11). The specifically postmodern importance of the Holocaust has been suggested thus: "The crime of Auschwitz as the moment of the accomplishment and self-destruction of [the] Enlightenment" (Albert Wellmer, "Metaphysics at the Moment of its Fall", trans. Shaun Whiteside in *Literary Theory Today*, ed. Peter Collier and Helga Geyer-Ryan (Polity Press, 1992), p. 35).

13. Paul Johnson, *A History of the Modern World: From 1917 to the 1980s* (Weidenfeld and Nicolson, 1984), p. 395. In later years Plath remained acutely aware of socio-political issues. Note for instance the "collage ... of postmodern culture", showing Plath "immersed in war, consumerism, photography and religion at the very moment she was starting to write the *Ariel* poems" as described in Rose, *The Haunting*, p. 9.

14. For his unease about this point, see D. M. Thomas, *Memories and Hallucinations* (Gollancz, 1988).

15. Miller, *Doubles*, pp. 318–28.

16. *Free Associations* (FAB, 1989) 17, pp. 135–9.

17. A. Alvarez, of course, argued she did not in *The Savage God: A Study of Suicide* (Weidenfeld & Nicolson, 1971).

18. T. S. Eliot, *The Complete Poems and Plays* (Faber and Faber, 1969), p. 196.

19. For descriptions of Plath's successful struggle to perfect her style see Axelrod, *Sylvia Plath* and Rose, *The Haunting*, in particular.

20. For her poem on such an execution see "The Trial of Man", *Collected Poems*, p. 312.

21. For this aspect of Plath's writing see Rose, *The Haunting*, pp. 165–204 and p. 173 in particular. It strikes me that this fantasy fable aspect of some of Plath's most striking poems is similar to those "petits récits" which Lyotard sees as politically subversive. See Jean-François Lyotard, "Lessons in paganism", in A. Benjamin (ed.), *The Lyotard Reader* (Blackwell, 1989).

5

John Berryman's "Henry"

In the "Dream Songs",[1] written between the mid-fifties and late sixties, Sylvia Plath's foreshortened career (along with the careers of other such poets as Theodore Roethke, Randall Jarrell and Delmore Schwartz) is memorialised as an instance of the artist's desperate fate in the contemporary world. Song 172 is entirely focused on Plath's death:

> long falls your exit all repeatingly,
> a poor exemplum, one more suicide
> to stack upon the others
> till stricken Henry with his sisters & brothers
> suddenly gone pauses to wonder why he
> alone breasts the wronging tide.
>
> (101)

Whereas in the extraordinary "Homage to Mistress Bradstreet" Berryman had sought to dramatise his verse as aesthetic dialogue between New World foundations and a postmodern American writing position ("reactor piles wage slow upon the wet brain rime") – a romanticised species of historiographic metafiction – in the songs an existential allegory of "Henry" is constructed where individual pilgrimage is subsumed into a larger group-project, a "family" imperative ("sisters and brothers") to live and work creatively in unpropitious times. Towards the end of the sequence, as the protagonist sails for Ireland, such friends and "friends of friends" are evoked as "labile souls" pursuing "insights" and embodying the wind which "blows hard from our past into our future" (Song 282, 214) – riders of process, the minstrels and the prophets of what we term postmodernity. Implicit here is a high ideal of the poetic function (owing principally to W. B. Yeats) which from the standpoint of the nineties must appear over-ambitious, if not *hubristic*. Yet it is the cost, not the glory, which the poet makes elegiac and to which he would quite shortly succumb – one more "poor exemplum", waving a languid farewell as he plunged from the Mississippi Bridge onto the frozen bank below: his own "resignation from us now" (101).

If the ontological anguish evident in Berryman's life and work is scarcely more acute than that expressed in, say, *The Waste Land* (1922), nevertheless the "Dream Songs", as much as Plath's *Ariel*, confirms a powerful myth of the contemporary poet's doom. The primary posture is not so much "alienation" (the cliché of normative modernity) as outrage and active anger; as the first song has it, "It was the thought that they thought / they could *do* it" (3). In such a line the historical situation becomes personalised (and demonised) as the "other". But "they" scarcely exist as meaningful entity (for all the poet's political indignation at times) and so the antagonist can be apostrophised another way: "I'm cross with god who has wrecked this generation" (Song 153, 82). Yet the result is the same: "We suffer on, a day, a day, a day". Berryman, one might feel, protests too much, for if we place the emotive protest "under erasure" for a while, the songs in fact depict a contemporary campus world of peculiar privilege – martinis, Mozart, chicken paprika, LSD, "delicate ladies / with ripped-off panties" (373, 305) and "my heavy daughter" (last words of the sequence, 317). The anguish is all in the head – yet no less real for that: for the mental world of the poet (himself depicted on television) is one of information implosion where atrocity appears pandemic – "the Armenians, the Jews, the Ibos" (353, 285) – leading to a sense that "culture was only a phase" and a Yeatsian "savagery" becomes the postmodern norm. "Culture", for Berryman, constitutes a lost ideal of High Art; in the "electric age" ("who has been running – er – er – things in recent – ech –/ in the United – If your screen is black", "The Lay of Ike", 23, 25), the poet feels contemporaneity as chaos. Hence, the dream in "Dream Songs" is, in fact, nightmare (even where Displacement renders this funny) and the public sphere becomes interiorised as alcoholic terror:

I am, outside. Incredible panic rules.
People are blowing and beating each other without mercy.

Drinks are boiling ....

(46, 50)

The poet becomes frenzied textualiser of a postEnlightenment, post-Gutenberg realm of hyperreal stammer: "Millennia whift and waft – one, one – er, er ..." (*sic*).

Against such ruin the poet shores up a codic eighteen-line verse unit which holds tight (despite some bold variations) in each of the three hundred and eighty-five songs (plus many more "uncanonical" songs both published and unpublished). Each song is typically split up into three stanzas of six lines – frequently lashed together by radical *enjambement*. Such triadic cellularity operates as an approximate rhythmical grid within which the dire self-questioning and weird argot of the wilder songs are played out. Despite some numerological game playing,[2] it seems unlikely that threeness is intended to convey any magical (or theological–trinitarian) import here; its peculiar affectivity merely resides in the almost organic authority of the primary number in-itself. Indeed, its formulaic consistency can induce a kind of structural hypnosis which the occasional exception oddly serves to deepen, if anything. Altogether, the linear regularity of the "Dream Songs" both contains the turmoil of postmodernity as represented in the protagonist's fraught existence and simulates the tropic form of electronic information (the exacting time slot of the News or game show) and the habit-forged work schedule of the toiling writer alike. Laid out in bold linear blocks in the original edition of *77 Dream Songs*, the triadic eighteen-liner becomes Berryman's mature poetic hallmark – both programmed procedure and expressionistic repetition-compulsion that measures out the postmodern as iterative symmetry. It accords not only with basic mathematics but also with the primal structures of subatomic physics (" – *Three quarks for Muster Mark!*").[3] Its effect is to ground the protagonist's weird and wayward Song of Himself in a cunning chicanery of ultimate order.

"Henry" is, of course, a canny fictive (and linguistic) construction – a caricatural existential site of contemporaneity, variously denominated by such game names as Pussy-cat, Mr Bones or Hank Hankovitch. Henry is a bit like Joyce's "HCE" (and can pun like Joyce) and while seeming to resemble the bearded Magus John Berryman (as photographed on the back-jacket of Faber and Faber's edition of *His Toy, His Dream, His Rest*), he can also, at times, appear as anarchically metamorphosic as, say, Ted Hughes's later "Crow". "Henry" constitutes Henry-as-zone and in this he contains multitudes. He is both a hyperreal projection of the poet's personality and a screen scan of his cultural environment – a compound simulacrum of the postmodern intellectual male (for Henry is very male – even masculinist). We are first introduced to him when he is in a massive sulk – "Huffy Henry". This is a mood which will recur, but it is by no means his only posture. For Henry has many roles and moods: he can appear, for instance, as teacher, barfly, rebel, hospital patient, traveller, famous poet, student, husband, singer, tax payer, father, son, scholar or lover and manifest a range of emotions between fear and facetiousness, gloom and perkiness, guilt and assertiveness or murderousness and tenderness. In most things he is excessive ("Mr Bones, / you makes too much / demand", 64, 71) – the poet's hypobolic phantasm of his own possibilities, a fictive gallimaufrey of self-parts in stridently rhetorical cry: "cagey John" (51, 55) here self-knowingly a prolix and extravagant orchestrator of voiced utterances against Silence.[4]

For "Henry" represents not just a character but also a linguistic field and herein lies much of Berryman's contribution. What a baffled Robert Lowell termed "Henry's queer baby talk"[5] is scarcely that at all – though Roethke's approximation to child speech[6] may well have been influential in its creation. The language of the "Dream Songs" constitutes a carnivalisation of the differences between discourse genres – the literary and the demotic, "ofay" (White Man) idiom and the Blues, textuality, orality and the electronic sound bite. It attempts to create a distinctive idiolect out of the babbling voices of the "electric age" USA – and, hence, remains virtually incomprehensible to the surviving defenders of a versified "Standard English". Here, for instance, is the last stanza of the second song:

> – Sir Bones, or Galahad: astonishin
> yo legal & yo good. Is you feel well?
> Honey dusk do sprawl.
> – Hit's hard. Kinged or thinged, though, fling & wing.
> Poll-cats are coming, hurrah, hurray.
> I votes in my hole.
>
> (2, 4)

Throughout, this apparently psychotic word salad stands in strong contrast to attempts elsewhere to assert a traditional poetic "voice" – "Hell is empty. O that has come to pass / which the cut Alexandrian foresaw" (56, 63 – here the myth about Origen is taken literally).[7] The second song is titled "Big Buttons,

Cornets: the advance" and is known to have been alluding to Daddy Rice's "Jim Crow" act in the early nineteenth century. So the lines do not even attempt to simulate actual African–American idiom but rather create a pastiche of a dated musical hall parody of Black South speech habits. Hence, "Is you feel well?" ("Does you does or does you don't take Access" is a recent advertisement appropriation of the same idiom). The next line is perhaps not ethnically specific (in a Southern context) – yet "dusk" is ambiguous and the sentence may, anyway, have a Joycean connotation ("Ah dew! It was so duusk that the tears of night began to fall"[8] – for "fall" see "sprawl"). "-Hit's hard" could well be mere pungent pun, but if the *Finnegans Wake* allusion holds so might Wyndham Lewis's parody of Joyce's style in *The Childermass*, which also alludes to "Jim Crow" acts: "hit's hit hit in me brain-pan and bin an mixt all the lettas!".[9] "Kinged" has a particular resonance in the years of the Civil Rights Movement (Martin Luther King), while the whole phrase sounds rather Gerard Manley Hopkins. J. M. Linebarger refers the next line to the song "Dixie"[10] but the line rhythm surely replicates that of "the Campbells are coming?/Hurrah, hurrah" – a Scottish song often used as a reel. So "Sir Galahad" resolves into an African–American democrat ("Poll-cats", "I votes"), with "hole" maybe to be heard as "hall". Yet the above remarks are inevitably speculation; they are sprung from Berryman's auditory collage where the traditional meditational line breaks down constantly into the near-random sound fills of some manic disc jockey. As in Joyce's *Wake*, the "electric age" is rendered as a textuality where any monological intent dissolves into carnivalesque dialogism.

The language of the "Dream Songs" – never satisfactorily accounted for by Berryman's critical admirers – can best be theorised, I believe, in such Bakhtinian[11] terms. Mikhail Bakhtin's notion of "dialogism" accords well with the heteroglot verbal wrangling which characterises the songs overall. Most important here are three basic emphases: the centrality of a responsible ("answerable") self, a consequent awareness of some dialogic "other" (in particular, that "friend, never named, who addresses [Henry] as Mr Bones and variants thereof",[12] but also the super-addressee of the poet's readership) and a "polyphonic" verbal environment (American campus speech as melting-pot) out of which the songs endeavour to assert some kind of authorial consistency "as if the worlds would answer to a code" (285, 217). Literary theories, such as Bakhtin's, are at their most useful when they can help to unpack specific literary practices – as is the case here. I shall consider each of the main emphases in order.

The selfhood of "Henry" is posited, *ab initio*, within an existential dynamic of "Self and Others".[13] As noted, Henry is introduced in contrast to "they" – *les autres*, seen as enemies, but the first song also establishes a fuzzy relation between Henry as "he" and the singer as "I" which suggests a duality of selves even before the advent of the "friend" in Song 2. In the general sequence, the drift between first, second and third persons,[14] the address to God, friends (especially other poets), the "friend", the poetic subject himself and the reader, plus a habit of sudden "quotationality" – all work together to construct a dynamic of answerability where the protagonist exists not as a monad among objects but as a (speaking) term in a relational complex whose main address is "I and Thou".[15] As Michael Holquist has written about Bakhtin's dialogism, "the self is like a sign in so far as it has no absolute meaning in itself: it … is relative, dependent for its existence on the other".[16] This is pretty much Henry's case. While he is typical of "modern men" who are "so saturated with self-consciousness that they seem to wander the world alone alienated from themselves and their culture",[17] this in itself becomes a subject of inter-relational utterance, negotiation and liminal dialogism. Such two-way interchange can be evidenced from a single line – "Are you radioactive, pal? – Pal, radioactive" (51, 55) – but more often it appears as more extensive self-declaration, suddenly cut into by a sardonic or comforting counter-voice. "Henry" constitutes a self seeking self-definition among other selves – including those of reader reception:

> …Henry was a needer
> of a very few or even of one of reader.

> (296, 228)

It is the variable position of "otherness" which reinforces the fluidity of Henry's selfhood. He may be termed "Sir Bones" or merely "Cat". For the others in the world of the songs are potentially infinite – friends or enemies, men or (idealised) women, the living or the dead. And against this perception of otherness, the picaresque development of Henry's saga is continuously played out: "– Come away, Mr Bones" (77, 84) is a condition of Henry's ability to "move on". So, as in psychoanalytic interpretations of dreams, the centrality of the dreamer is all-important but can only function in terms of fantasy scenarios of the others to which s/he relates in terms of projection or introjection. And, as in the theory of dreamwork, the others may spring from everyday experience (both professional – "Hey ... assistant professors, full" – or intimate – "I loved her and she killed me"), for all that their roles in the songs may be quite fantastic. Such others mainly constitute Henry's parents and offspring, artistic friends or heroes, desired women, the imagined readership and God. The last term cannot be merely rationalised in, say, a Freudian "translation" if we are to take Berryman's contribution at all seriously. For some of the profoundest poems are "Confessional" in the Augustinian rather than the poetry-fashion sense and represent a mode of discourse more akin to prayer than psychic or social expressionistic revelation. At the same time, the utterance may bear cultural rather than private resonance: "Dinch me, dark God" (266, 195) speaks back to Donne and a whole tradition of pious self-examination[18] as well as out of existential selfhood – and toward the Divine. The other here partakes of "a vast congeries of contesting meanings, a heteroglossia so varied that no single term capable of unifying its diversifying energies is possible".[19] Otherness, like selfhood, is ultimately a function of the shared possibilities for utterance immanent in the poet's inherited language and culture.

The heteroglot characteristic of the "Dream Songs" is both a triumph of creative performance and a stumbling-block for the conventional reader. Even when restricted to the English language it strays over all kinds of boundaries:

> Sire, damp me down. Me feudal O, me yore
> (male Muse) serf, if anyfing;
> which rank I pull.
>
> (58, 65)

Mediaeval pastiche and modern slang, Donne, Hopkins and *Finnegans Wake* – such lines wholly rebut the remaining prejudice for some "true voice of feeling" as unified idiolect (for example, the "line" of Frost, Larkin or early Heaney). Of course, Berryman is not alone in employing such poetic "polyphony" – *The Waste Land* and the *Cantos* had prepared the way and David Jones's *In Parenthesis* can deploy even more shifts of idiom. What all such "makars" share is Bakhtin's sense that the richness of a linguistic environment matters more than any utterer's mono-logical intent and that live language both addresses and is addressed. The "Dream Songs" makes this a central principle of Berryman's expressivity and thereby articulates a culture, as well as a personal "case". To do so the poet utilises, among other devices, "allusions, clichés, puns, neologisms, changes in parts of speech, ellipses, syntactical inversions, variety in levels and kinds of diction".[20] This makes for a notably idiosyncratic mix-ture of language habits where an arcanely allusive high style is shot through with street slang and cocktail party Europeanisms. However, at the centre of this linguistic farrago is an ongoing dialogue between the key poles of US cultural tension in the fifties and sixties – African–American modes of orality (in-cluding musical Jazz, Blues and Soul elements) and WASP middle-class literariness (with the weight of Western tradition underpinning it). As already mentioned, both poles are rep-resented typically through parodic devices: it is not that Berryman articulates a satisfactory "Black voice" or a consistent "White voice" but that he makes exemplary for high culture an uneasy commingling of utterances from both national poles:

> The high ones die, die. They die. You look up and who's
>   there?
> – Easy, easy, Mr Bones. I is on your side.

>   (36, 40)

Out of such bizarre dialogue the songs assert a fantasy of fellowship between Black and White where the former has the greater experiential strength: one of the most repeated and characteristic words of the sequence is "pal".

Through this self-caricatural dialogism, then, Berryman builds up his "Henry" as an allegorical figuration of American post-modernity. The songs effect a kind of *Pilgrim's Progress* – except that progress here is rather process: not salvation but endurance is the aim, with death as both antagonist and the horizon of self-definition. There is no more purposive schema here, I believe, than in, say, Pound's *Cantos* or Williams' *Paterson*. Aristotelian beginning-middle-and-end, the classical paradigm for the project of modernity, has itself become passé – has come to *its* end. The songs are postmodern through their "electric age" return to a (pre-Socratic) Heraclitean flux – relativistic, existential, heterogeneous. In Song 293 Henry disavows plotting ("cliffhangers or old serials") and "ultimate structure" dissolves into "according to his nature" (*His Toy*, 225), a chronotope[21] of "abstract adventure time" ("one million & thirteen falls") with only gestural structure markers – seven parts in two books (but then there are the apocrypha left over), the "Op. posth." fourteen songs (quasi-epic descent into the land of the dead) or the culminatory voyage to Europe and return to his house "made of wood". Song 261 (190) expresses the sequence's portentous open-endedness and dour sense of an ending:

> We're circling, waiting for the tower & the marker
> the radio's out, some runways are brighter
> as we break Control & come down with our size.

Yet descent or resolution are not effected in the sequence itself; it could continue as long as the poet had the will to write (along with his "heavy daughter"). To end the sequence where Berryman did was a publishing decision not structurally necessary to the "Dream Songs" as such. Joel Conarroe is absolutely wrong in discerning an "absolute ... sense of closure".[22]

"Henry" is a type of postmodern man (not woman – though Sylvia Plath might have warmed to him): we could allegorise him as homo schizophrenicus (Ihab Hassan had labelled postmodernism schizophrenic as early as 1971).[23] In Berryman's characterisation, reality and phantasy, the personal and the political, élite allusion and demotic speech habits are bizarrely interfused. And because Henry's story embodies no real sense of direction (death here constitutes a synchronic rather than a diachronic dimension), beginnings and endings in the sequence appear as highly fictive try-outs – from a "rational" standpoint, an ultimately psychotic "gaming" which plays with the narrative linearity of modernity in a situation where that can scarcely apply. Although the character's rehearsal of strategies is extreme, his condition seems posited as normative – in the sense that he represents what Richard Rorty has termed the "pageant of historical progress which will gradually encompass all the human race",[24] without, however, this being felt as purposive for the individual. Henry represents the privileged free soul, but as Sartre emphasised "condemned to be free"[25] with the anguish this entails, in a postmodern world of competing (and protesting) voices, obligations and desires. "Henry" is a site of restlessness. Berryman's fictive zone of words constitutes the contemporary as frenetic aspiration, terror and conscience in perpetual struggle. Such a construction is hyperreal in that it is surely as false as it is true and as applicable as it is rebarbative. "Henry" becomes a schizophrenic characterisation of human awareness and agency almost pornographically uncovered to the reader's gaze and response. In him is elaborated a psychic striptease (sexy sexism and the culturally forbidden *frisson* of the Holy together), frantically exposed to a readership still mostly at home in restrained literary convention, within a rapidly accelerating world of electronic over-information.

Song 45 (49) expresses one kind of provocative excess in the realm of Berryman's sequence. It commences with the brilliant dead-pan line: "He stared at ruin. Ruin stared straight back". The poem conforms strictly to the overall pattern of eighteen lines split into three stanzas of six lines each, with subtle variations of rhyme scheme in each case: a b b c a c, a b c c b a, a b c b a c. Such formality sets up an aesthetic frame within which imagination and ideas weave a *danse macabre*. The projected relational dynamic of protagonist and "ruin" as "old friends" becomes distorted, at the end, by the emergence of a stranger (ruin-for-real, as it were) who calls the bluff of the whole scenario. Henry's escapades involve raw sexuality, jail-house blues and electrotherapy experience; they switch between home-truths and some "Asian city", they include somewhat random misadventures in which the word "crossed" (rhymed with "lost") is repeated three times. The detritus of modern civilisation – papers, telephone, wiring – becomes implicated in false judgment ("Epileptic"), loneliness and disillusionment. Through Berryman's familiar facility with common jargon and his canny construction of a shadowy thriller-*dénouement*, the lines build up a Kafkaesque scenario of incomprehensible failure and potential hurt wherein the self's accommodation with slow self-destruction is wholly undercut and danger attains a new and unexpected visage. The rhythm is jerky and insidiously urgent, the grammatical form essentially paratactic; the rhyme-words are predominantly monosyllabic. The poem ends with the stark encounter and with a nodding gesture of recognition. But the last "word" is as surprising as it is shocking – "un-" (*sic*).

Song 114 (41) threads a single ""Mr Bones" intervention into Henry's third/first person complaint. "In trouble" again, our anti-hero evokes the fabular figures of Mr Past, Dr Present and Sir Future Dubious as spectral presences attendant on Henry's wry self-reckoning. Perhaps partly invaded by the speech idioms of the interlocutor, the main idiom becomes, as often, waywardly idiosyncratic. Towards the end there are some jokey discordances in the play of *difference* ("weft" for left or "wives" for lives). The formula "livey toads" is a slick variation on Lewis Carroll's "slithy toves", while Wilfred Owen is restored to his captain's rank in an estranged version of "move him into the sun". Such defamiliarising strategies signal both a crisis in signification and a mordant anguish in the represented selfhood. It is likely that the two are dependent on each other since "Henry"'s predicament is, throughout, that of the lord of language in an era of polyglot schmalz and populist culture. The resultant idiolect is worked out of both polarities, as in the phrase "wherefore I pines". The Germanic "ich" is deployed almost as boldly as in Plath (but without the hypnotic reiteration), while the exotically archaic "I can no foothold here" – the compound noun suppressing potential verbal energy – reminds us of the studied erudition which underlies all Berryman's verse. "Pluck Dr Present" speaks quite obviously for the language-conscious self-estrangement that is exercised throughout. Berryman's attempt to shore up frag-ments against ruin is typically expressed here as linguistic fantasticality. In ways, it can appear forced and self-indulgent, yet the condition it speaks for is, I believe, as much cultural and personal. "O" in line 5, as elsewhere in the "Dream Songs", can be understood as representing astonishment and dismay at the same time – while holding out an expressive lifeline to the reader also. Altogether, the poem effects an eighteen-line protest against Dr Present as perceived by articulate agency. The final Owen allusion constitutes a "quotational" attempt to find precedents – if existentially a self-indulgent one: the truer conclusion is expressed in "May his chains bask".

The dialogical "antagonist" gets the last word in Song 223 (152). This plays with Henry's identification as "Pussy-cat": cats

are represented as agile movers, men as devious and guilty –
"Henry", of course, is a compound of both. The poem tends to
collate the words "miserable" and "mysteries" within a historical
search for some meaning of meaning. There is a Yeatsian
assertiveness in the poetic evocation of the dawning of human
consciousness: "springy for pride". Yet this is set within a
"later", postmodern situation ("this tick of time") where gloom
and despondency appear endemic. But such a description belies
the poem's energy and slick wit. Line lengths are dazzlingly
various, sudden questions perforate Henry's overall peroration,
misery is set in opposition to wonder and the zany comparison
of human and feline realities, as well as the dialogic statement
and reply, render the piece a comedic exercise in Jacobean
gloom. Once again the eighteen-line, cellular, three-part format
is adhered to strictly – the rangy, speaking voice straddling such
structuration with casual yet poignant speculation. And, again,
the dominant voice both sets up an idiomatic contrast to the
interlocutor's and at times appears to have introjected the speech
habits of his "shadow". The poem negotiates oppositions of
nature and culture, darkness and light, ecstasy and agony,
reality and concealment – I and Thou in a wry interrogation of
Being: "Why? Who? When?" The questions resemble those of
Beckett's *The Unnamable*. As the interlocutor suggests, Henry
enquires too much. Such things are not to be known. Put another
way, orality (either primary or secondary) may have little
patience with the metaphysical tortuousness of the highly
literate consciousness. Out of such a torsion the predicament of
postmodern information overload is played out.

Song 238 (167) is entitled "Henry's Programme for God",
which seems to foreshadow some of the song-titles in Ted
Hughes' *Crow*. It also represents one of many meditations in the
"Dream Songs" where there is no "cork"-faced interlocutor and
the dialogic wrestling of discourse is set against Divinity as
super-addressee.[26] The poem begins with assertive responses to
quoted formulations of failure. The protagonist claims immunity
from such put-downs, yet immediately queries the meaning of
existence in-itself. The ensuing figuration of God renders
Divinity as akin to Yeats's "rough beast", here identified with
Goya's late, nightmarish etchings. Yet even this frightful personification is expressed as a "Thou" appealing for the "thud of
love". God should be restrained, the twelfth line suggests. The

final sestet homes in on human response to the metaphysical conundrum and a neo-Yeatsian final question which memorialises the Spanish painter's courage and queries the ontological identity of the *daemon* which drove him on. In fact, the poem constitutes not only a dialogue with God but a summoning of and conversation with at least two artists – the "gay" Yeats of his later Nietzschean phase and the last "touch of paranoia" in the painter ("paranoia" tellingly rhymed with Goya). Such a scenario inevitably pits Berryman's Romanticism (and his residual Roman Catholicism) against his incipient "postmodernism", and thereby makes visible some of the major cross-currents within the condition of postmodernity. "Paranoia" here, in fact, links the painter with the God of the poem – first by rhyme then by grammar. Once again, the hyperreal fantasia of "Henry" (where persona/e and world are woven together by dreamwork) is set against some ultimate where signs become wonders and metafictionality is subsumed in Word. But as elsewhere in the "Dream Songs" and in, too, at least Auden, Ginsberg, the Plath of "Mystic", Hill and R. S. Thomas, it is the "cloud of unknowing" which is most emphasised – that and human qualities of questioning and endurance.

Overall, Berryman's extended sequence (and the uncanonical songs can be included here) constitutes a poetic exhibition of quirky brilliance but one which, for all its individuality, nevertheless provides a print-out of postmodernity – if only in black-and-white negative. The "Dream Songs" are codic formulations of a personal "periplum"[27] of the contemporary, *in extremis*. Like Ginsberg's poems, they are emanations from the prime locus of the postmodern – the USA between the fifties and the sixties. The writing position is (almost inevitably) of the *élite*, the campus world where since the Second World War, in particular, poetry has become sacralised as authentic *parole* in an era of media rhetoric. Yet the songs speak to and integrate within themselves a variety of class and ethnic registrations – most especially a theatrical "poor-Black" voice – and so offer a provisional mapping of what a United Nations postmodernism might look like, that is, dialogical, sometimes conflictual, heterogeneous but ultimately policed by structure – as demanding as it can be variable. The terrain covered is partially (hence, by extension, potentially) world-wide and because "Dream" precedes and constantly informs "Song", at issue are also, possible and alternative worlds. In this Berryman's verse both (largely) foreshadows and parallels those novels of the American sixties and seventies or the British seventies and eighties, which have been confidently constituted as postmodernist fiction. The "Dream Songs" have long offered a cornucopia of strategies and techniques for the literature of postmodernity.

Altogether, Berryman's mature poetry represents a unique combination of existential anguish and heteroglot self-consciousness where the pressures of contemporaneity are unforgettably put into play. And this poetic "gaming" is fully in accord with the ideas of Freud, Piaget and Gregory Bateson which Patricia Waugh astutely brings to bear in her book on postmodern fiction.[28] Like so many commentaries on post-modern writing, Waugh's text exclusively expounds facets of recent novelistic practice. Yet much of what she has written would apply to Berryman's tricky fictional self-referentiality and language games. Her comment that "the paranoia that permeates the metafictional writing of the sixties and seventies is ... slowly giving way to celebration, to the discovery of new forms of the fantastic" (p. 9) is suggestive of the Berryman of the late fifties and mid-sixties not in terms of chronological development but of the polarities already inherent in his work. For in the "Dream Songs" paranoia and celebration co-exist as "schizo-phrenic" registration of the postmodern condition in a variable balancing act. The world of "Henry" is funny – but it is also agonistic and fraught with metaphysical dread. Berryman's play is dexterous, but inherently dangerous – for as in Plath's case, writers are liable to pick up the existential tab of the phantasies they give expression to. In the last instance, the songs constitute a wager where Pascal and indeed Augustine are more to the point than "Adlai mine" or "Ike". In this they set postmodernity within a long historical agenda which makes the Enlightenment project, itself, only one stage (if a highly significant one) in some unfolding of a cosmic dialogism. The allegorical "Henry" will survive the poet's own demise to continue to demand: "Why? Who? When?"

Notes

1. To my knowledge, there is no collected volume of Berryman's poems. The volumes I have used are: John Berryman, *77 Dream Songs* (Faber and Faber, 1964); *His Toy, His Dream, His Poems* (Faber and Faber, 1978). For the first seventy-seven songs my page numbers refer to the first book; thereafter, up to song 385 the page numbers refer to the second book.

2. "*His Toy, His Dream, His Rest* is divided into four books of 308 Songs (308 is four times 77). The four books have, respectively, 13, 53, 132, and 106 Songs. We can note all kinds of mathematical possibilities: 13 is one-half of 26, 132 minus 106 is 26, 106 is twice 53, and so on." J. M. Linebarger, *John Berryman* (Boston, Mass.: Twayne Publishers, K. Hall & Co., 1974), p. 82.

3. James Joyce, *Finnegans Wake* (Faber and Faber, 1939), p. 383. The physicists' word "quark" was, of course, appropriated from this context.

4. I am guessing that Berryman is also playing off the name of the composer John Cage whose best-known work was called *Silence*.

5. Quoted by Linebarger, *John Berryman*, p. 168.

6. Especially in the cycle of six poems from *Praise to the End* (1951).

7. Cf. "The story, told by Eusebius of Caesarea on hearsay evidence, that in the enthusiasm of youth Origen castrated himself to ensure chastity, could be true ... But when Origen himself expounded Matt XIX, 12 ('there are some who have made themselves eunuchs for the kingdom of heaven's sake') he strongly deplored any literal interpretation of the words. Perhaps Eusabius was uncritically reporting malicious gossip retailed by Origen's enemies, of whom there were many" (Henry Chadwick, *The Early Church* (Penguin, 1986), p. 109).

8. James Joyce, *Finnegans Wake*, p. 158.

9. Wyndham Lewis, *The Childermass* (John Calder, 1965; first published 1928), p. 173.

10. Linebarger, *John Berryman*, p. 87.

11. It is interesting, in this regard, that the reception of Bakhtin's ideas and the theorisation of postmodernism occupy approximately the same recent time period.

12. Berryman, *His Toy*, preliminary "Note".

13. I have in mind, of course, R. D. Laing, *Self and Others* (Tavistock 1961) – a contemporaneous work by the sixties' psychoanalytic guru.

14. "Henry ... talks about himself sometimes in the first person, sometimes in the third, sometimes even in the second." Berryman's "Note", *His Toy*, ..., IX.

15. Bakhtin, at least, knew Martin Buber's *I and Thou* – perhaps Berryman did too. My copy was translated by Ronald Gregor Smith (Charles Scribner's & Sons, 1958).

16. Michael Holquist, *Dialogism: Bakhtin and his World* (Routledge, 1990), p. 35. I have relied mainly on this work for my remarks

here although I have read three of Bakhtin's works in translation and have often discussed his ideas with my colleague Graham Pechey. See especially Graham Pechey, "Bakhtin, Marxism and Post-structuralism" in *Literature, Politics and Theory: Papers from the Essex Conference 1976–84*, ed. Francis Barker, Peter Hulme, Margaret Iversen and Diana Loxley (Methuen, 1986), pp. 104–25.

17. Holquist, *Dialogism*, p. 74.
18. See, for instance, Patrick Grant, *The Transformation of Sin: Studies in Donne, Herbert, Vaughan, and Traherne* (McGill-Queen's University Press, 1974).
19. Holquist, *Dialogism*, p. 14.
20. Linebarger, *John Berryman*, p. 121.
21. Bakhtin's word: see especially Holquist, *Dialogism*, p. 120.
22. Joel Conarroe, *John Berryman: An Introduction to the Poetry* (Columbia University Press, 1977), p. 91.
23. See Connor, *Postmodernist Culture*, pp. 111–12.
24. Richard Rorty, "Cosmopolitanism with Emancipation: a response to Lyotard", in *Modernity and Identity*, ed. Lash and Friedman, p. 68.
25. Jean-Paul Sartre, *Existentialism and Humanism*, trans. Philip Mairet (Eyre Methuen, 1978), p. 34.
26. "If there is something like a God concept in Bakhtin, it is surely the superaddressee, for without faith that we will be understood, somehow, sometime, by *somebody*, we would not speak at all". From the Introduction to M. M. Bakhtin, *Speech Genres and Other Late Essays*, trans. Vern W. McGee, edited by Caryl Emerson and Michael Holquist (University of Texas Press, 1986), p. xviii.
27. "Periplum" or "periplus" was Ezra Pound's term in the *Cantos* to suggest navigation in terms of practical knowledge. See, for instance, Alan Durant, *Ezra Pound, Identity in Crisis: A Fundamental Reassessment of the Poet and his Work* (Harvester Press, 1981), pp. 48–9.
28. Patricia Waugh, *Metafiction: The Theory and Practice of Self-Conscious Fiction* (Methuen, 1984).

6

Ted Hughes' "Crow"

Crow[1] (1970) is probably the most jarringly innovative cycle of British poems written since the Second World War. It decisively parts company with the naturalistic "empiricism" through which Hughes' career was launched and it has learnt enough from North America (both the breakthroughs of Ginsberg or Berryman and American–Indian and Eskimo mythology) to carve out new imaginative terrain, where filmic cartooning and tribal creation-tale spring a sport as drastically reductive as it is inventively brilliant. One can only guess what the precedent of his wife's work and death might have contributed to this "surviving guy's"[2] high-speed, black-and-white fabulation of postmodern awareness. Certainly, the "crackle and drag"[3] of darkness informs his scenario of neo-Darwinian struggle, played out against a cosmic backdrop like some grotesque shadow-puppet show. The trappings of postmodernity are here in terms of rocket-launches, high-speed car adventures, anatomical reductionism of bodily functions and a sense of apocalypse thrown into relief by the glare of red violence. The sequence's affective power is a product of "secondary orality" where *"petits récits"* become genesis myths and mini-scripts of disaster, radical parataxis boils rationality down into the bones and blood beat which contrived it and primary rhythm becomes as insistent and hectic as the raunchiest ritual. *Crow* effects a return of the "savage god"[4] (for all its theatrical and often comical agnosticism), where the postmodern is screened in bold, typographic blocks as eternal recurrence of psychophysical violence and violation. Crow constitutes an appallingly stimulating *tour de force*.

The figure of Crow has its "evolutionary" origin in Hughes' earlier depictions of hawks, thrushes and pike.[5] "Hawk Roosting", from *Lupercal* for instance, exemplifies a naturalistic treatment of the bird-predator which nevertheless has its analogue in the human world of late modernity – as in Auden's thirties' juxtaposition of "hawk" and "helmeted airman".[6] The hawk is situated in its typical environment, "the top of the wood". What it "dreams" of is a red-in-claw extrapolation of its feeding function: "My manners are tearing off heads". However, such zoological reductionism is complicated by the poet's use of the dramatic first person (for example, "I kill where I please") and by an accumulation of highly socialised terms – "falsifying", "rehearse", "convenience", "advantage", "inspection", "produce", "revolve", "manners", "allotment", "argument", "permitted" – which connects the hawk's natural hunting habits with the geopolitical aggressiveness of the century of two world wars and countless smaller wars. The "empirical" bird is evoked to operate as a brutal symbolisation of evolutionary rules and modern history alike. Hughes' defensive comment that "what I had in mind was that in this hawk Nature is thinking".[7] scarcely squares with the implication of much of his diction. At the same time, the egoic personification at the end seems remote from the actual natural realm, however jaundiced one's view of the food chain:

> My eye has permitted no change.
> I am going to keep things like this.

This is malign teleology masquerading as natural science. The "pathetic fallacy" consists here in a poetic projection of "narcissistic",[8] masculinist aggression onto a predator outside of the moral frame. For all its somewhat stagy coldness and ruthlessness, this is an effective poem, yet it contrives to yoke by violence together two incompatible worlds[9] – the worlds of natural history and geopolitical histrionics. Ultimately, it rings a little false because *realpolitik* and *samurai* hubris intrude into the would-be objective realm of animal observation. The poem remains rooted in a postwar British positivism (the natural habitat of Larkin, Amis and Robert Conquest), where linguistic tropes are meant to mirror reality, when its imaginative vision is potentially in search of more dynamically expressive signification.

The *Crow* volume solves the problem almost at a stroke.[10] For here Hughes elaborates an "idea of a style"[11] where "super-simple and super-ugly language" is in the service of a quasi-mythological imagination, creating poems which "challenge the everyday assumptions of our language".[12] In "A Disaster", for instance, it is precisely positivist language – the discourse of Will To Truth as Will To Power – which is blighting the planet:

There came news of a word.
Crow saw it killing men ... /
He saw its excreta poisoning seas ... /
He saw its breath burning whole lands ....

(28)

Against such irresponsible, logocentric scientism Hughes pits an ironic and highly metaphorical "pop poetry" style (perhaps owing to Ginsberg, as to, perhaps, contemporary European protest poets)[13] founded in paratactical primary orality and appropriating the language tropes of Fleet Street, the movies and street talk. Oscillating between speech and literariness, the stylistic effect can be quite unique:

'A final try,' said God. 'Now, LOVE.'
Crow convulsed, gaped, retched and
Man's bodiless prodigious head
Bulbed out onto the earth, with swivelling eyes,
Jabbering protest – ...

(Crow's First Lesson, 16)

The language of the Crow sequence constitutes a flagrant counter-discourse to the positivistic, rationalising monologism of Western master narratives. It flaunts its dynamic alogicality in terms of *ostinato* rhythm, radical repetition, agglutinative phrasal units, imagistic explosiveness and parodic allegorisation. It can also be boldly "quotational" with respect both to the non-scientific discourse of religion and that of high literature: "In the beginning was scream" ("Lineage", 10); "Never/Never Never" (*ibid.*). Hughes' linguistic strategy throughout the book represents a flamboyant rebellion against contemporaneous British poetic language and Western scientistic discourse alike.

We are today in a better position to evaluate Hughes' "mythological" turn against cultural positivism in the late sixties. What could once have been seen as mere neo-Romantic "shamanism" or neo-"primitivistic" anarchism may now be reinterpreted as a prophetic expression of an ongoing shift in intellectual culture at large. Here, for example, is a contemporary sociologist writing about state-of-the-art social theory and practice:

Irony is a powerful device precisely because in reversing the presumably real order of things it calls everything, including the order of things, into question. It is, therefore, risky business ....

The ironist position, therefore, breaks with what Rorty (1989) calls the "Plato-Kant canon". It does not concern itself with the general truth, goodness or beauty of things. Philosophy since Hegel and Nietzsche through Heidegger to Derrida is replaced by literary criticism ....

In this sense, irony is the discursive form of postmodern social theory.[14]

The anarchic irony in *Crow* is precisely of this kind, employed by a poet who was also a trained anthropologist but had broken with the "modern" discursive and methodological assumptions of this discipline long before social science had discovered "postmodernism". Charles Lemert, whose words I have just quoted, goes on to elaborate an anthropological[15] critique of George Marcus and Michael Fischer (1986) where the historical phenomenon of Captain James Cook's death is described from the Hawaiian mythic point of view. "The narrative focus", Lemert writes, "is not so much *on* the early nineteenth-century Hawaiians as it is *from their perspective*" (26). The implications of this in terms of "dialogism" as well as irony are clear. Lemert continues to suggest "one of the deepest effects, aesthetic and political of postmodernism is to disrupt one's sense not only of the true and the false, but of the present and past, and all other modernist dichotomies" (32). He concludes his essay by affirming "the ironic centrality of differences in a decentred world" (42). Thus, have both the "Trickster" and the god Hermes together invaded the disciplines which hitherto had made them mere "objects" of scientific knowledge. *Crow* is a major precursor of this (highly controversial) shift in social theory.

For what the entire *Crow* project accomplishes is an ironic (and irreverent) recasting of any Enlightenment narrative of human history, in terms of a pastiche mythological sequence of poetic fables. Creation tales are less imitated than recycled through cartoon conventions and pop imagery. Thus, Keith Sagar's[16] worthy attempt to extrapolate Hughes' achievement as some Lawrentian return of Romanticism precisely misreads the proleptically postmodern character of *Crow*. We have here not Dionysius restored but Hermes in the guise of postmodern harlequin. For "primitive" tale-telling is consistently exercised in terms of contemporary imagery and diction: "He jumped into the plane but her body was jammed in the jet – / ... the flight was cancelled" ("Crow and Mama", 13), "there was this garbage can, bottom rusted away" ("Crow Alights", 17), "the earth shrunk to the size of a hand grenade" ("Truth Kills Everybody", 69). So the "tribal" feel of these dramatic mini-narratives pertains less to the camp-fire than to the global village. The cosmic intent of North-West American–Indian fabulations about the Raven or of Winnebago Trickster tales (as described by Paul Radin),[17] is projected backward and forward over the entire terrain of known or imagined planetary history to rewrite the "March of Progress" in terms of discrete, comi-tragic allegorical fables. Neither the sequencing of the Crow poems in the volume nor the Ur narrative which Hughes has provided in his readings[18] seems to me structurally important, since one poem appears to breed another in quite random ways and at issue is not only linear discursive logic but also the Western Aesthetic as structure-in-itself. So versified tale-telling here is essentially a pragmatic device – not a rival mode of "Truth": ironic affect rules and "Truth" itself is seen as what "kills everybody". This is art as postmodern play, illuminating reality precisely by foregrounding the "serious" murderousness through which modernity had tried to order its world:

Its mishmash of scripture and physics,
With here, brains in hands, for example,
And there, legs in a treetop ...
Till ... /
... what was left looked around at what was left.
("Crow's Account of the Battle", 21–2)

The figure of Crow (who is like the dark side of Auden's Ariel) is central to the whole conception and affect. I have suggested that he is a postmodern harlequin and this takes us so far – for although unrelentingly black there is a shimmering and ambiguous quality to him (he can be contemplative and even ruefully compassionate as well as robotically cruel); at the same time he has a magical quality, a pantomimic role and a touch of genuine devilry.[19] However, to really account for his characteristics we need look also

to more contemporary populist caricatures, such as Tom (in "Tom
and Jerry"), Puddy-tat, the joker in *Batman* or the ubiquitous
personification of malignity in the Rolling Stones' *Sympathy for the
Devil.* Crow is both cosmic and marginal, perpetrator and victim,
trickster and butt, sadist and philosopher, animal and spiritual
principle, actor and observer: in short, he is a dynamic, free-floating
signifier loosely uniting a sequence of tragi-comic allegories about
life, the universe and everything. Above all he is a survivor – if
necessary by cartoon instant-recreation after some moment of
annihilation. And throughout he is markedly masculinist – a
caricatural personification of the male "lethal weapon", arrogant,
destructive, with an endless egoic appetite. Only in his "Undersong"
can his opposite, the "feminine", be voiced somewhat in its "own"
terms.

   Crow reads like some checklist of postmodernist techniques as
identified in accounts of recent prose fiction. "Historiographic
metafiction" is here achieved as a radical rewriting of human
history from the Creation to the Great War ("Crow's Account of the
Battle", 21–2) and the age of the Hydrogen Bomb ("Notes for a
Little Play", 72) through a slangy pastiche of creation myths.
Allusions to the Bible or Dante (with a sly parody of Eliot's later
style – "Will this cipher divulge itself to digestion / Under hearing
beyond understanding", "Crow Communes", 25) co-exist with
comic-cuts technique, Hammer Horror shock effects and slapstick
in a bizarre mélange of low and high style. In a sense, the whole
constitutes "Yorkshire" Magical Realism, for the actions are as
surreal as they point to realities and illusionist tricks such as rapid
metamorphosis are frequently employed. The "zone" is com-
pounded of a particularly European history set on an aboriginal
plane which scrupulously obeys the edicts of Social Darwinism.
The language is spare, paratactical, image obsessed and as
insistently rhythmic as a backing track. As allegorical scan of the
postmodern world, *Crow* is more instantly accessible (especially
when *heard*) than most postmodernist novels and, in many ways,
more disturbingly incisive. For all its Hughesian quirkiness, *Crow*
represents, I suggest, the most typically postmodern British poetry
most of us know of.

   However, Hughes' fictive irony is not merely "depthless", for all
the brilliance of its surface. For both the ubiquitous activity of Crow
and the mythic implosion of creation-history-apocalypse allow the
expression of a holistic ecological vision appalled at the ravagement

of the planet. Crow is a postmodern figure because – for all his own lethal greed – he stands as shocked witness to the global destructiveness of human history as modernity. This is the case in his battle accounts, for instance. With respect to "St George" this is inscribed on a more personalised plane – the "knight" (a scientist and mathematician, it appears) hacks up his wife and children in a frenzy; in "The Battle" the focus is on the political level – modern warfare and violence in general as overeasy habit. In some poems Crow is not present (for example, "Revenge Fable", 58) and the personal and the political are merged: the "person" on the "topmost twig" represents humanity itself as summit of creation. But the figure attacks and destroys his "mother" (Nature) with "disgusts / Bulldozers and detergents". The result is cautionary: "His head fell off like a leaf". In one of the most arresting poems of the sequence, "Truth Kills Everybody", Crow himself stands for over-inquisitive and over-grasping humanity. Crow holds onto Proteus, as Odysseus had done, but the truth he seeks turns out to be highly explosive: the last metamorphosis of the "old man of the sea" is as a global hand grenade. It blasts Crow to "nothing". The implication is obvious – yet no less chilling for that.

Hughes' saga of the human infringement on the ecosphere combines the twin perspectives of psychoanalysis and geopolitical history. In the first case, some of Hughes' work for Peter Brook's production of Seneca's *Oedipus* has strayed into the sequence, as with "Song for Phallus" (63).[20] However, elsewhere the broadly Freudian perception of the root of civilisation's discontents is imaginatively incorporated into the whole by making Crow mischievously complicit in the division of the two sexes (as in "A Childish Prank" or "Crow's First Lesson", 15 and 16). From this primal struggle come birth, Oedipal rage and subsequent spurning of the mother. Hughes' psychoanalytic vision pertains almost wholly to male derangement and this in turn is linked to social and intellectual masculinism in the geopolitical sphere, which is represented as a scientistic (and sometimes psychopathic) assault on Mother Nature herself: "He pounded and hacked at her / With numbers and equations and laws / Which he invented and called Truth" ("Revenge Fable", 58). If the psychoanalytic component can be seen as mere cultural inheritance, Hughes' projection of this into a critique of "Will to Truth" and the entire project of modernity was prophetic. These poems were written in a decade when phrases like "the white heat of technology" still had dazzling political power and any effective Green Movement was years away. If Romanticism (partly mediated through Robert Graves) underlies Hughes' vision, the allegorical black humour and filmic cartooning whereby he expresses it are distinctly of the postmodern era.

The most representative and I think effective poems in the sequence are those either in which Crow is a participant or which are attributed to him (as opposed to "Owl" or "Eskimo"). "Crow Alights" (17), for instance, is a quite chilling "filmic" exercise in moving from cosmic panning to dire close-up. Crow is very much the detached observer here; he can blink (and does) but he has no interactive role in the "evidence". The initial scan links the earth's mountains and ocean with God's "spores" – the stars in the nothingness of space. The sight is chilling to Crow who senses an activity immanent in the apparent stasis. This potential is almost instantly translated into an unravelling catalogue of drained, metonymic details – clothing, face, cigarette, cup. The glimpsed figure in its silent house is linked associatively with the detritus of civilisation swept by the wind on the moor. The figure could be thinking – at any rate it is unmoving except for the motion of smoking, itself perhaps as index of man's propensity for poisoning himself and his world through his habits. The scenario is not apocalyptic, but it is wholly desecrated. It is notable that Crow as notorious scavenger (celebrated elsewhere when he guzzles ice-cream) can find nothing to eat here. He is merely a recorder of ruin and the verse cannily rehearses the sense of cosmic entropy, ending in human desolation, by disintegrating the longer sentences of the initial exposition into a series of short, bleak phrases and sentences lacking even in verbal connectives: "Near the hand, this cup". What had begun, for all its cool distance, in metaphorical rhetoric resolves into colloquial, static metonymy. The scene cannot "escape" Crow because it has no energy left: Crow remains as a kind of camera, taking snapshots of postmodernity as waste land.

By contrast, in "The Black Beast" (23) Crow is both dynamically engaged and a representative of human activity seen as dehumanised scientism. The Beast itself is a kind of "Lord of the Flies" – a demonised Other, an enemy and Alien. Here psychoanalytic "splitting" conjoins with a caricatural "Rise of Science" to effect an eschatological end-scenario. Crow hunts the hated Other to the point of cartoon disappearance in pursuit of the stars. Originally-sottish brutality develops into calculated anatomisation of corpses in the pursuit of the unformulatable goal. Cain, Nero[21] and clinical analysis come together in the gaudily melodramatic line: "Crow killed his brother and turned him inside out to stare at his colour". But Crow's atrocities are not yet over. He wilfully transforms the planet into a burnt-out "clinker" and then projects himself into outer space in the same futile pursuit. Throughout, the rhythm of the poem replicates the crudest ritual chanting – each further attempt of Crow sprung from variants on the same base-line (and unanswerable) question: "Where is the Black Beast?" The action ends on its artificial, fast-forward trajectory (slickly parodic in this) yet the enduring question remains to haunt the reader. The poem might be seen as mere cartoon-surface ironic postmodernism, yet it surely sketches out a genuine fear – the fear that contemporary civilisation is out of control, as reckless and self-obsessed as the all-licensed Crow.

"The Battle of Osfrontalis" (29) develops the irony in "A Disaster", aimed at logocentricity ("a word"), into a vivid panto-mime of Crow's resistance to the postmodern degeneration of "Word" into commercial and political litter-letter formulae and jingles. Thus, words assail him in terms of insurance policies, warrants and blank cheques. Crow adopts an instinctively different (and appropriate) response in each case – playing mad, dead or just doodling. When words come as a magic lamp he sells it to buy a tasty treat of food. When they come as "vaginas in a row" (mechanistic pornography appealing to a private furtiveness) his defence is clubably masculinist: he invites his friends – presumably to inspect them in derision and lewd hilarity. Later on in the poem, words attack him in terms of their verbal suggestivity – glottals, aspirates and consonants: Crow remains indifferent, as an actual bird might be to a radio stammering unattended at the edge of a field. Crow's tactics triumph. The words take refuge in a Yorrick-like skull, a notable reversal of the economy whereby Hamlet transmutes bright bone into "philosophising". In doing so the words withdraw the "whole world", in the sense of human lin-guistic constructions of the planetary reality. The *Ding an sich* shows no interest at all: it goes on as before. And so does Crow, after a yawn; only the skull could be of interest to him, but he had picked it clean long before. Throughout the poem Crow's vital evasiveness is in strong contrast to the aggressive persistence of the words, which insist on plopping into his consciousness like a succession of junk mail. In a story-line highly typical of the Crow sequence, an accumulation of strangely metamorphosic manifestations leads to a showdown – here resolved as anticlimax. Crow, as allegory of natural instinct, has triumphed over the harassment of man-made culture reduced to officialdom and consumerism as meaningless ad-speak. "Crow took a sip of water and thanked heaven": this line might represent the only intelligent *human* reaction, too, in the represented world of fatuous linguistic hyperreality.

However, in "Crow Goes Hunting" (45) our protagonist tries siding with culture over against nature in the form of a hare. In effect, the hare represents Crow himself in his more usual role. In this instance, Crow summons up words for himself ("Clear-eyed, resounding, well-trained"). Such words resemble (if not embody) the positivistic project of controlling things through constructing a "Mirror of Nature".[22] The words pursue the hare, "resounding". Hare's response is that of instant adaptation. S/he becomes progressively a bunker, a flock of birds, a rainshower, an earthquake and finally a hare again (having eaten the persecutory words). Crow has used words aggressively throughout (perhaps out of fascination with the strategies used against him in "The Battle of Osfrontalis"): his words hunt, become bombs, shot-gun pellets and finally turn into a restraining reservoir. Neither assault nor restraint succeed. The hare's ingenuity of response is as effective as when Crow used his instinct against similar cultural persecution. Throughout, the action is played out as a typical "Tom and Jerry" game and counter-game, the "little guy" the victor, natural resilience shown as superior to verbal meddling. Yet Crow, having backed a loser, is generous in his temporary defeat. He gazes after the hare (rather as D. H. Lawrence once appreciated an untamable rabbit),[23] "Speechless with admiration".

"Crow Blacker than ever" (57) shows Hughes' versatile protagonist as mock mediator between man and God. At the beginning of the poem there is set up a strong mutual antipathy between the divine and human realms. God is "disgusted" with man and vice versa; the former thus retreats into heaven and the latter finds refuge in his woman. This sets up a cosmic disintegration which Crow decides to mend in his own way – by nailing heaven and earth together. The process of nailing, of course, alludes (ironically) to the crucifixion of Christ: Crow, as it were, acts as the malign spirit joining man to God through suffering and death. So is effected a parodic version of Incarnation:

So man cried, but with God's voice.
And God bled, but with man's blood.

This indicates the extent to which, for all his ironic "anthropologising", Hughes' imagination remains steeped in the central theological scenario of Christianised Europe. However, it is a scenario which the poem labels "gangrenous" – not a means of redemption but a spectacle of horror. The fates of God and man are so fixed together that neither can retain individual identity: the blurring becomes an "agony". The poem begins to peter out in two-word, then one-word, lines of radical, grammatically split emphasis. Yet Crow, typically, exults in the feat he has performed, seeing it as an act of outstanding creativity: a true *acte gratuit*. So Crow plays the clown as existentialist: morality is neither here nor there; self-assertion through ruthless completion of the self's project is all that matters. As grotesquely as a figure sketched by Gerald Scarfe, Crow preens himself on his own perverse vitality: "flying the black flag of himself".

In "Crow Improvises" (53) the improvisation could be read as the working-out of the poet's own life and career, including the invention of this entire sequence of poems – Crow mythologised as the daemon behind the Hughes legend. The "man" we are introduced to is himself a balancer of "sun" and "leaf", "ancestors" and "the battle of the Somme", "gravestone", "baby's ... molar", "Relativity" and "the bible". Out of the clash between such heterogeneous contraries comes "the spark" which both sears a "name" into being and scours being into "ashes". Most of the properties named typify the poetic themes of Hughes' career to this date. There is particular poignancy, in such a reading, when the child's tooth is set alongside the "girl's laugh" and an evoked "seven-year honeymoon" ("Seven years, if you want to know").[24] Unlike his first wife's work, Hughes' poetry rarely strikes one as subjective; on the contrary and as is the case in most of this sequence, whatever might have a "personal" origin becomes subsumed into a coolly objective scenario. However, coded references are visible even in as overtly an "omniscient" and impersonal modern writer as James Joyce.[25] "Seven years" is as much a shared (and number-magicalised) legend as a lived reality. In the poem the lost honeymoon leads to smitten testicles and whitened hair. After this the "improvised" subject weighs birth against death and flies away (with creator-Crow?) into "Screams, discretions, indiscretions etcetera" – which might serve as one kind of description of the *Crow* poems themselves.

A final example, "Crow's Undersong" (47), indicates that the raw and ironic masculinist vision of the sequence exists as a pragmatic construction of postmodern realities, projected in cartoon-mythological fables, from a position of far broader (if not "deeper") awareness. The poem speaks what Crow cannot utter – what is both "Other" to him and a condition (if only by binary opposition) of his scandalous self-assertion. Crow is shown to have a violent way with any kind of "Mamma", yet here the "she" cannot be finally ignored if life, let alone "city", is to exist at all:

> She comes with the birth push
> Into eyelashes into nipples the fingertips ....

The feminine ("Mother Nature") is associated with water (which in "Crow and the Sea", 68, humiliates our protagonist and in "HOW WATER BEGAN TO PLAY", 79, simply "wanted to live"). Sixteen lines in this twenty-three-line poem begin, hypnotically, with the word "She". It is arguable that the feminine here is itself a caricature, as Crow is. If so, it is overall an appreciative ironic representation: "She has come amorous it is all she has come for". There are many things, the poem tells us, that "she" cannot do: but she simply *is* – and because of that there cannot be "no hope". If she brings tears then that is because living includes tears, but she also brings warmth and fruit. There is little point in merely privileging (as "life-enhancing") this delicate, accumulative lyric over the black allegorising of most of the *Crow* poems, but the volume would lack more if it were excluded than is the case for any other one poem. It offers a benign space of deconstruction for the brilliant but macabre game rules of *Crow's* fabulatory reductiveness.

In his (liberally "postmodernist") book *Contingency, Irony and Solidarity*, Richard Rorty quotes with approval John Dewey's words:

> ... imagination is the chief instrument of the good ... art is more moral than moralities. For the latter either are, or tend to become, consecrations of the status quo .... The moral prophets of humanity have always been poets even though they spoke in free verse or by parable.[26]

Despite its shock effects and at times its affected superficiality, I take Hughes' *Crow* to be morally prophetic in very much this sense. Rorty's book is postmodern precisely in the way it rejects "theory" as totalising and favours poetic "redescriptions" as illuminations which have no palpable intent on the public domain. This, I think, is the case with *Crow*, which is poetic through using both radical free verse and quite drastic parable. The sequence rewrites both theological and "rational" history through a caricature anthropology which, however "depthless" the trope, alerts us to ultimately moral dangers in the ideas and actions of our era. For Crow, himself, represents especially a fantastical figuration of that Death Instinct and blind egotism which inheres in the postmodern technological assault upon the life forms of the planet. Indeed, Crow is no more a bird than was the roosting hawk – though the verse now shows itself more aware of this. The sequence, *Crow*, not only rewrites the narrative of human destiny (a kind of History of the World in 60 Short Fables), it also rewrites the poetic discourse and cultural dominants in which Hughes' career was founded in the fifties. In Rorty's terms, *Crow* rewrites both the "Plato–Kant canon"[27] and the callow British positivism of "The Movement" era in terms of Hughes' own fantasy, stylistic aplomb and fictive inventiveness.

As with Berryman's *Dream Songs*, I do not think we need to take the sequence, as published, with too much seriousness. Keith Sagar has shown that some cognate material has been left out[28] and it could well be argued that some rather extraneous poems have been kept in. Conscious sequence structuration (and the packaging of poetic publication events) become themselves "naturally" deconstructable in the culture of postmodernity. But the poetic method at work in the *Crow* text – its stylistic risk-taking, narrative force and parodic cartooning – expresses aspects of some new realities we live in, increasingly, with each year that goes by. The Vietnam War, the rise of Monetarism, the failure of the Brandt Report, the Presidential election of a minor Hollywood actor, the Falklands Campaign, the starvation in the Horn of Africa, the metamorphosis of Cold War into East European competing nationalisms and the increase in the hole in the ozone layer – all these phenomena can be seen more credibly in terms of *Crow* than, say, in terms of Dante's *Inferno*, Shakespearean comedy or Wordsworth's *Prelude*. If *The Waste Land* is a precedent ("Burning / burning / burning", "Crow's Last Stand", 67), Hughes' phraseology, filmic method and ironic intent are wholly his own creation. The poems provide a brash but penetrating way of looking at the contemporary. And so it is not surprising that R. S. Thomas[29] took them as a springboard for his own later, *via negativa* interrogation of postmodernity *sub specie aeternitatis*.

Notes

1. All references are to Ted Hughes, *Crow: From the Life and Songs of the Crow* (Faber and Faber, 1970).
2. John Berryman's phrase for Hughes, after Sylvia Plath's death, in Song 187, *His Toy, His Dream, His Rest*, p. 116. Berryman wonders "what he makes of it": *Crow* might be one kind of answer.
3. From Plath's last line: "Her blacks crackle and drag": in "Edge", *Collected Poems*, p. 273; cf. "blackening dregs" in "The Horses", *The Hawk in the Rain* (Faber and Faber, 1972; originally 1957), p. 15. This first collection is dedicated "To Sylvia".
4. W. B. Yeats's phrase. Hughes was greatly influenced by Yeats's life and verse.
5. See, for instance, "The Hawk in the Rain", Ted Hughes, *The Hawk in the Rain* (Faber and Faber, 1972, originally printed 1957), p. 1, "Hawk Roosting" and "Pike", Ted Hughes, *Lupercal* (Faber and Faber, 1961), pp. 26 and 56–7.
6. "Consider", W. H. Auden, *Collected Shorter Poems 1930–1944* (Faber and Faber, 1962, p. 43). It strikes me that *Crow* boldly epitomises that flattening of "the human subject to a viewing eye and devouring stomach" which Terry Eagleton hypothesises as a function of late capitalism in *Ideology: An Introduction* (Verso, 1991), p. 38.
7. Quoted from an interview in *London Magazine* (1971) by Terry Gifford and Neil Roberts, *Ted Hughes: A Critical Study* (Faber and Faber, 1981), p. 69.
8. Quite obviously so, but see the argument about traditional Western poetry, in general, in Antony Easthope, *Poetry and Phantasy* (Cambridge University Press, 1989).
9. I had Karl Popper's distinctions in mind: for example, between world 1 (material things and objects) and world 2 (motives and feelings, etc.). See Karl Popper, *Objective Mind: An Evolutionary Epistemology* (Clarendon Press, 1972).
10. There are, of course, precedent poems like "Reveille" and "Theology" in Ted Hughes, *Wodwo* (Faber and Faber, 1967), pp. 35 and 149.
11. Quoted by Gifford and Roberts, *Ted Hughes*, p. 102 from the *London Magazine* interview.
12. Gifford and Roberts, *ibid.*, p. 126.
13. For example, Zbigniew Herbert, Miroslav Holub or Vasko Popa. See Gifford and Roberts, *ibid.*, p. 131.
14. Charles Lemert, "General Social Theory, Irony, Postmodernism" in *Postmodernism and Social Theory*, ed. Steven Seidman and David G. Wagner (Blackwell, 1992), pp. 22 and 23.
15. George Marcus and Michael M. J. Fischer, *Anthropology as Cultural Critique* (Chicago University Press, 1986).
16. See Keith Sagar, *The Art of Ted Hughes* (Cambridge University Press, 1975 and 1980).
17. As quoted in Sagar and Gifford and Roberts.
18. For a description of these see Gifford and Roberts, *Ted Hughes*, pp. 115–16.

19. *Chambers English Dictionary* suggests French "harlequen" may be cognate with Old French "Hellequin" – a devil in Mediaeval legend.
20. See Gifford and Roberts, *Ted Hughes*, p. 103.
21. Nero was reputed to have ripped open his dead mother's womb to see where he had been born.
22. I am thinking of Richard Rorty's book, *Philosophy and the Mirror of Nature* (Princeton University Press, 1979).
23. See "Adolf", *Phoenix: The Posthumous Papers of D. H. Lawrence*, ed. Edward D. McDonald (Heinemann, 1967), pp. 7–13.
24. From Sylvia Plath, "Daddy", *Collected Poems*, p. 224.
25. See, for instance, my *Intertextual Dynamics*, pp. 125–32 and 158–65 for personal references to Lewis, Pound and Eliot.
26. Richard Rorty, *Contingency, Irony and Solidarity* (Cambridge University Press, 1989), p. 69.
27. *Ibid.*, p. 96.
28. Keith Sagar, *The Art of Ted Hughes*, pp. 101–45.
29. See below Chapter 9.

7
Geoffrey Hill's "Mercia"

"Genesis", the first poem in Geoffrey Hill's *Collected Poems* (1985),[1] constitutes one of the most apparently self-confident declarations in recent writing in English. First published in the pamphlet *Fantasy Poems 11* (Fantasy Press, 1952) and then in *For the Unfallen* (1959), it asserts a cosmic vision of the creation story from the poet's post-Holocaust standpoint of prophetic wrestling:

> Against the burly air I strode
> Crying the miracles of God.

As in the biblical narrative, the process of creation is here split into six stages or "days", but here the sixth day includes both the fall of humankind and our (ambiguous) redemption. In the first stage, sea and land are brought together to energise the salmon's striving; in the second and third, the law of "tooth and claw" unites the osprey and the ferret; in the fourth, "myth" is invented as a dream of "immortality" to stand against mere physicality; but in the fifth there is a move away from the realm of "phoenix" back to flesh and blood. So, in the last stage, the human predicament is heralded as an incarnational struggle between human clay and transcendence:

> By blood we live, the hot, the cold,
> To ravage and redeem the world.

The lines introject verbal power from major poets[2] in the tradition to effect a quasi-ironic, but gristly strength of line most unusual for so early a production. From the standpoint of the fifties (World War is surely hinted at in the "close shrouds" of drowned sailors), Hill attempts to sum up the entire human project as a fable of struggle, loss and reparation played off against the earliest Middle Eastern myths.[3] The poem strikes one as Romantic in terms of the prophetic role of its declared persona, but postmodern in its self-conscious inscription of prophecy as a strong but quasi-ironic recycling of the myths and poetic voices of the past.

However, unlike Hughes in *Crow*, Hill's main poetic vehicle will not be creation myth or fable as such, but verse meditation in dialogue with the annals and poems of the European past and in the case of his "Mercia", prose "hymns" where history is mingled with personal stages of maturation in an *"outre monde"*[4] created through deft and wryly comic, "versets".[5] "Requiem for the Plantagenet Kings" exemplifies the meditational mode, in a Baroque[6] rhetorical display which serves to undermine artistic construction itself in the face of the absolute "sea": "They lie; they lie; secure in the decay / of blood". This is a version of "Arundel Tomb"[7] where what will survive of us is guilt: "blood-marks, crowns hacked and coveted". The poem moots a "trial-day" of final Judgement. The point here concerns less Hill's personal belief[8] than how history is to be read *sub specie aeternitatis*. Here the "lie" of "well-dressed alabaster" impacts on the word "alight" – suggestive of both revelation and purgatorial incandescence: the latter meaning, in turn, looks back to the earlier ambiguous phrase "being fired", where pride is seen as an engine of the whole Mediaeval, dynastic wrangling. As often in Hill, (and with Eliot's Phlebas and "The Dry Salvages" as precedent), the sea constitutes an ultimate horizon. "Dead" is the last word of the poem – as death, perhaps, is what separates the ongoing struggles of life from "history" or process from traces. The marks of "history" here constitute their own form of rigidified hyperreality – in search of some absolute grounding in justice and judgement.

Such engagement with the factitious nature of historical inheritance will also animate the last poetic sequence in the book, "The Mystery of the Charity of Charles Péguy" (1983) – which may yet prove to be Hill's most celebrated production. Although Péguy's life and death stand much closer to us than the protagonists of "Towton ... / Wakefield, Tewksebury" (71) or even "Shiloh" (65), the gulf between reality and inscription remains open to the probing of "historiographic metafiction".[9] Here the traces are modern – to be filtered through postmodern modes of representation:

The brisk celluloid clatters through the gate;
The cortège of the century dances in the street....

(183)

But the "jolly cartoon" includes Péguy's *Cahiers*, the contextual "new farce" *Sleepers Awake* (to set against Ibsen's *When We Dead Awaken* – Hill has been a translator of Ibsen) and the relationship between Péguy's propagandist nationalism and Jaurès' assassination. In a somewhat parodic rewriting of Marx's famous commentary, we are told that: "History commands the stage wielding a toy gun, / Rehearsing another scene". In the evoked filmic context, the French soldiers, Péguy among them, are punningly evoked as hyperreal chimera – "reeling" toward the front and its very real disasters. In the last poem of the sequence (10, 195–6), the same historiographic sifting of the "last rites of truth" remains where the eloquence of Marx is fused with the elegiac brilliance of Ezra Pound in "Hugh Selwyn Mauberley": "Low tragedy, high farce, fight for command". Both "éloge" and "elegy" are emanations from the uncertain borderline between the realms of "Truth and Calliope"[10] which is nevertheless the battlefront too where actual social constructions collide, ambitions battle each other and men really die – as Péguy died. "Still mourn", the poem tells us, for the last word is not about epistemological uncertainty or the gap between word and world but about the fact that history is made, people die, in the midst of and out of such ambivalences.

In *"Mercian Hymns"* (1971) Hill postmodernises the realm of Offa by constructing a prose "dream-time" which represents the soul's voyage through the shards of history to attempted rendezvous with a remembered "present". It constitutes a chastening vision of "Englishness" whose unresolved problematic concerns precisely "the Presence of the Past" – the title given to the "postmodernist" Venice Biennale of 1983. Hill's unique and idiosyncratic space–time collage is displayed in the opening interpellation:

> King of the perennial holly-groves, the riven sand-stone: over-lord of the M5: architect of the historic rampart and ditch, the citadel at Tamworth, the summer hermitage in Holy Cross: guardian of the Welsh Bridge and the Iron Bridge: contractor to the desirable new estates: saltmaster: money-changer ....
>
> (105)

Rooted in a verbal cragginess reminiscent of Basil Bunting's work (and with an evocation of "Great Time",[11] within an intimate geography, similar to that in *Briggflatts*), Hill's quirky juxtaposition of holly-groves and M5, rampart and Iron Bridge, "summer heritage" and "desirable new estates" immediately establishes a fictive realm where "Mercia" becomes as resonant (and problematic) as Allen Ginsberg's "America". The whole apostrophe (concluding with reference to Offa's relationship to Charlemagne) begins to sound like Borges' wonderfully transcategorical "Chinese encyclopaedia".[12] It ends, dialogically, with Offa's imagined response, which surely owns its "mass culture" kinship to Humphrey Bogart's well-known one-liner in *Casablanca*: "sing it again".

"Mercia" is a zone where the traces of history and the strains of personal maturation are indissolubly linked: "On the morning of the crowning we chorused our remission from school" (107). Hill's Mercia constitutes the English Midlands as paradigmatic of the historic island story (and "Albion" did indeed make lorries). The focused time-in-point ("entre deux guerres", as Hill's master had put it, but including World War Two itself) is remembered from a postmodern moment where "telephones", "car-dealers" and "confetti" have become widely shared social indices. "Mercia" is summoned up "in tapestries, in dreams" (127) but it leads to one end, where aeroplanes, archaeology and incipient ecological environmentalism ("snout intimate with worms and leaves", XI, 115) mingle in insistent conjunction. "Mercia" is very much an "outre monde" where no Pilgrim Fathers can attempt a cancellation of "history" in terms of some "God-blessed" modernity, where the repressed of tradition returns and the universal is only to be found in the rooted particular:

Gran lit the gas, his dice whirred in the ludo-cup, he entered into the last dream of Offa the King.

(XXIX, 133)

The name Mercia denotes an ancient kingdom ruled by more than one Offa, but Hill's ear-wise scrupulosity no doubt is aware that his sequence plays also with the implications of "mercy" and "*merci*". "Mercia" represents an England, an Englishness, blessed, thankful, even in its violence, its ravagement ("Gasholders, russet among fields", VII, 111), its "clash" of diplomatic activity and its perennial yearning for economic stability ("rare coins", XIII, 117). "Mercia" becomes a plane of transhistorical struggle where failure sinks back into "mud" and success, is, at best, a "master-mason"'s skill, the peaceful exchange of a two-edged sword or the consolations of philosophy.

The history invoked in the sequence is real enough – as Hill's notes attest. As an undergraduate at Oxford, the poet "worked very hard at the orthodox English Language and Literature syllabus of that time"[13] and references to A. H. Smith's edition of *The Parker Chronicle*, G. Zarnecki's *Later English Romanesque Sculpture* or Dorothy Whitelock's *The Beginnings of English Society* show that a familiarity with standard works of historical scholarship underpins the (sometimes casual) imbrication of the past over his schoolboy experiences. Such scholarship may seem now to be "modern" in that it is as preoccupied with the demarcation of geographical borders as it is with the fixing of a firm currency. Dorothy Whitelock observes:

> ...Offa, reigning twelve generations before his famous Mercian namesake and descendent, was remembered as the King who established the Eider as the boundary between the Angles and the Swaefe, their southern neighbours in their homeland.[14]

Mercian Hymns is postmodern in that it inscribes the "processes of generation; deeds of settlement" (XXVIII, 132) as a relativistic process – as relativistic as, say, the murderous realignment of borders between Serbs, Croats and Bosnians in one-time Yugoslavia, at the present time of writing.

For Hill's sequence represents history as a kind of flux, uncertainly permeated by the waywardness of its actors rather than as any "March of Progress" or "Evolution of the Nation-State". One locus is the "earthy shelter" (XXII, 126) where a wireless broadcasts "battle anthems" and "gregarious news" – postmodern information fodder for a Second World War schoolboy "war-band", in its own way as tribal as the legends of Offa himself. Modernity, as rationalised written history, is bracketed out of this interpenetration of anarchic wargames: in twentieth century Europe, as in eighth century Mercia, "true governance" is a dream in a world "full of strategy". The simulacrum of Rule (precariously anchored to fact in terms of certain earthworks, artefacts or chronicles) becomes dispersed in the end ("he vanished", 134), leaving behind only coins and traces of mud. The "Presence of the Past" can only be apprehended through such evocative signs and the poems themselves operate only as "coins" and "traces" of both an English past and a now-lost boyhood and acculturation.

The vehicle used is somewhat bizarrely termed "hymn" (there may be a pun here, since the sequence very much expresses masculinist experience – hims ancient and modern, as it were). We are given the primary reference point of the Mercian Hymns in *Sweet's*

Anglo-Saxon Reader (as edited by C. T. Onions – "Sometime Reader in English Philology in the University of Oxford").[15] The Old English hymns constitute six texts from the "Vespasian Psalter", glosses on psalms, etc., in interlinear Anglo-Saxon and Latin. They seem to provide a stylistic benchmark for Hill's experimental venture. Hymn A commences:

> Lȳtel ic wes betwih broður mīne, ond iu[n]gra in
> Pusillus eram inter fratres meos, et acolescentior in
>
> hūse feadur mīnes
> domo patris mei.[16]

In section Vl (101) Hill "translates" this as "A boy at odds in the house, lonely among brothers". As Ezra Pound grounded the opening of his Canto l[17] in the primal alliterative line of Old English poetry so Hill simulates here the concrete simplicity of Old English prose. At the same time, the principle of interlinear languages sets a precedent for the etymological heterogeneity of some of Hill's sentences: for example, "ransacked epiphanies, vertebrae of the chimera, armour of wild bees' lavae" (Xll, 116), where the "mind of Europe" speaks out variously in Anglo-Saxon, Latin, Greek, Old Norse ("ransack") and Old French ("armour"). However, Hill's intent is not merely antiquarian and in temporarily forsaking the sternly ceremonious verse line of which he had already proved himself so capable, his *Mercian Hymns* open up the (more French)[18] tradition of poetic prose "versets" for exploitation in the less metrically aware era of English postmodernity. Not only is the rhythm of a different kind, so also may be the linguistic texture – that is, informal, paratactical, pared down to the semantic bone:

> Tumult recedes as though into the long rain. Groves of legendary
> holly; silverdark the ridged gleam.
>
> (XXVIII, 132)

As in the case of Ginsberg, behind such facility lie the hard-won experimentations of modernism – those of T. E. Hulme, Wyndham Lewis, Pound, Eliot, H. D. and David Jones, for example. The effect is to cut out unnecessary syntactical machinery, develop the sentence as a unit of expressivity rather than a grammatical contraption (subject–verb–object, etc.) and set individual words in auditory, rather than rational, space. For the "Sometime Reader" of post-modernity it offers a freer mode of evocation: "Candles of gnarled resin, apple-branches, the tacky mistletoe" (Vl, 110).

The sequence has no overall structural principle that I can detect – except, perhaps, as with Pound's *Cantos* or Ginsberg's "Wichita Vortex Sutra", to imply that deconstruction as collage can itself operate as structuration. *Mercian Hymns* commences with an invocation of Offa and ends with a valedictory fragment and there is a suggestion of maturation – being born, childhood, education, ruling – but narrative here is shrunken down to "petits récits" and vignettes and plotting is virtually non-existent. The whole cycle is post-Gutenberg in that it refuses those structural tropes of continuity, development and *rationale* which the print revolution,[19] most especially, had inculcated as the cultural mode of modernity. It exists as a collation of mosaic friezes (where each word constitutes a discrete, contributory "stone") or as a grouping of short film-clips (thirty in all) about a particular theme. There are two interwoven thematic motifs: the life and reign of Offa and the mythicised boyhood of the writing persona. But there is, I suggest, just one "hero" – "Mercia" itself. This zone is what holds the individual sections in place and gives the "hymns" an overall subject. It is a realm of both rootedness and fantasy, where nature and culture no longer operate as binary oppositions but implode into each other as part of one visionary manifestation.

The sequence grounds ecological holism in a specific geography where boundaries are still under negotiation and the phrase "Rex Totius Anglorum Patriae" (Xlll, 117) is consciously ironic. What underlies all is the reality of earthiness – habitat of mole and "red-helmeted worms" – nourishing element of holly-grove and nettles alike, recipient of spent bodies and preserver of cultural traces. The Mercian soil calls forth some of Hill's richest vocabulary: "telluric cultures, enriched with shards, corms, nodules, the sunk solids of gravity" (Xll, 116). Some of these poems read as genuine "Notes from Underground" – that is to say, not the neurotic despair of some modernist "Bohemian" but the nurturative éloge of a postmodern, sensuous environmentalist. The last word of the cycle is "mud" as the first is "King": the golden boy, as "staggeringly-gifted child" of whatever kind, comes from and returns to this loamy compound of water and dust. Both Offa and poetic protagonist are intimately associated, at various points, with the earth of Mercia; if the language inevitably partakes of "simulation", it points to something out of which the hyperreal itself is ultimately produced – "Ramparts of compost". And above this levelling plane, the sequence continuously decorates itself in greenness – grass, plants, shrubs, bushes, trees and their evergreen parasites, such as mistletoe. Earth is not here (as in the treatises of modernity) a global tract to be "mastered" and exploited but simply the thin mantle of organic nutrition which (alone) allows the possibility of any "culture" at all.

As already noted, the culture represented in the sequence is notably masculinist and is, to a degree, made ironic in almost these terms: "Merovingian car-dealers, Welsh mercenaries; a shuffle of house-carls" (XXVll, 131). Violence is incipient both in Offa's England and the protagonist's boy-world – where the counter to a Ceolred's carelessness is a vindictive flaying. And in so violent a world, the obsession of culture is with power, rules and stability. In this sequence coinage becomes even more a symbol of "governance" than the sword exchanged with the Frankish dignitaries. Hill seems to owe something to Pound's insistence on sound "coin, credit and circulation!"[20] as a basis for both good art and ordered society: in Xlll the metallic depiction of Offa ("the masterful head emerges", 117) is expressed through close allusion to the "Medallion" to Venus in "Hugh Selwyn Mauberley"; "The sleek head emerges ...."[21] Exactitude of likeness (as well as purity of metal) is what underpins the validity of coinage (the penalty for sloppiness is "mutilation", 115) and from this springs not only controlled trading but the value of the golden "hoard" (Xll, 116) and the possibility of accurate dating. Yet the postmodern irony of *Mercian Hymns* allows the reader to view this obsession with exactitude, consistency and coherent legitimation from quite a distance: in the end, Offa's coins become merely one more archaeological sign – rendered up to just such historiographic phantasmogoria as the poem overall creates. Like the dice in the ludo cup, the coins constitute a gamble of historical speculation not a foundation for some "science" of the past. So too the meditated edicts of the long-dead king provide few notes towards a theory of culture; Hill's overall scepticism renders them like the invoked blow of an axe, echoes of "lost sound".

But if history is not fixable, still it will not go away. The sequence is perhaps most identifiably "postmodernist" precisely in the way that the poetic protagonist's childhood cannot be cut off from the past in some framework of the "late thirties and early forties". "Mercia" is a mental space where Offa and aircraft co-exist – so too red dust and radio, Gran and Ceolred, holly, impetigo and gas-holders. Growing up into "Englishness" here constitutes both a refusal of the "modern" rationalisation of writing the past as mere causality for a self-sufficient present and the neoconservative construction of a sanitised "heritage", where civilisation grows from precedent to precedent. *Mercian Hymns* shows the mutual implication of past and present, the rootedness of both in the soil that nurtures them, the violence and uncertainty of all human culture and the fragility, as well as the pervasiveness, of power. "Mercia" is a palimpsest, where Ginsberg's "America" is a video scan: it is layered in etymological depth where history continuously writes and overwrites itself – in whatever language – compulsively recycling the signifieds of "ancilla" and "servus" (114) and inscribing the deeds of petty despots (whether kings or egotistical adolescents) who seek to dominate both. "Mercia", in addition, is a little like post-Cold War Europe and, hence, the sequence is prophetic as well as historiographic. It expresses precisely the tensions between federal dreams and bolt-holes of "subsidiarity", fantasies of "central bank" stability and fears that coinage is mere simulacrum, the fierce prides and suspicions which render borders dangerously fluid and turn friends into enemies and spill blood over "evergreen albums". After the dreams of modernity – world-empire, New World, the Marxist Internationale – "Mercia" is where we now live and, in a sense, always have lived.

Poem ll encapsulates the hyperreality of actual, space–time living by playing with a name. "Offa", we are told, is ultimately a name for conjuring (one could imagine the late Tommy Cooper using it thus in a "magical" gag). In his entry on Hill in *The Dictionary of Literary Biography*, Vincent B. Sherry Jr perceptively connects the poet's technique here with the quasi-acrostic conventions of Anglo-Saxon riddles. He suggests that the connections of the sound of the name with laughter, coughing, the initials of an organisation (an "Offa" we cannot refuse?) and a race start "all echo the unwritten letters o,f,f,a: sounds of laughing, coughing, the initials of an organisation, or offer, 'They're off!'."[22] The poem is generally riddle-like too in its radical brevity and the rapid accumulation of its suggestions. On the page, it is presented as three lines of brief nouns, most often deftly qualified, connected somewhat randomly by commas, full-stops and one semicolon (dashes might have done as well) followed by one line of two more noun compounds, after a typographical space. There is not a single conventional sentence in sight. The effect is to strand the riddling probes in grammatical limbo, rather akin to the recent advertising technique of Perrier's "eau/O" campaign on British television. The associative technique here takes us from familiarity ("pet-name") to the ironised oddity of conjuration. In between, the postmodern is evoked as possible brand-name, graffito and obsolete "phonograph". Before the sequence is established, a key naming is shuffled through a number of varieties of *difference* in terms of social carnivalesque. To the attentive reader, this sets up an ironic tone and intention as a key for understanding the whole sequence.

X collapses the figure of Offa into that of the poetic subject in terms of the history conscious and yet in ways timeless process of school-learning. The first verse is dominated by the fetishistic symbol of the desk and the personal appropriation of this through the sunken *graffito* of the individual name. The desk becomes an extension of the ego in its process of educational self-extension. In verset ll this is extrapolated as phantasies of omnipotence, where "the people" are the protagonist's charge, his slain rival requires forgiveness and "History" is a potlatch of mutual appreciation and diplomacy between himself and "the Muse". However, remorse rears its head in the next section and it is resolved only by recourse to the (actual or introjected) mother – "Tell me". The verset is elliptical, eloquent and gnomic even in its dialogical interchange, but it is also psychoanalytically canny and like Tiresias tells more than can be easily explained.

The concluding section of the poem constitutes an extraordinary vignette of boyhood in just thirty-two words. The external and inner realms of experience are expressed through a contrast between sunlight and dream, then pears and the pet cat summon up the sensuous immediacy of early youth before "shades of the prison house" descend in terms of the subtleties of Latin – not the "mother-tongue", but the universalistic language of identification, classification, understanding and control. Latin, here, surely becomes the ultimate origin and rationale of the project of modernity ("History") as experienced by the growing boy. It is placed against the oral realm of the mother (as post-Kleinian psychoanalysis will place abstract truth against emotional reality).[23] Here the "Muse" is acrostically close to the cat's name "Smut" [must?] and both, unlike history's "retributions", stand for "God bless".

XVI expresses uneasy negotiation – exchange of gifts between rival realms, Albion and the "Frankish" kingdom: rivalry strong enough to last considerably more than the next thousand years. The sword exchanged is a "crux", both phallic symbol and sign of surrender, "regaled" (hence, made regal too) with "slaughter". Meeting is modified confrontation – the incarnational acts listed and codified as exactly as in David Jones' *Anathemata*.[24] We are not told on which shore the salutation takes place, but a similarly Jonesian epiphany magically unites the two cultures – not just in the strife which divides them but also in terms of a similar natural and religious inheritance:

> Shafts from the winter sun homing upon earth's rim. Christ's mass: in the thick of a snowy forest the flickering evergreen fissured with light.

> (120)

So in Sherwood, so in the Ardennes. The poem moves to a vinous reworking of Eliot's reductive "Eating and drinking. Dung and death".[25] But where the poem differs from both Eliot and Jones (where, perhaps, it postmodernises the accomplished modernist practices of both) is in phrasal curtness, the abrupt slashing of syntactical flow and a gnomic, abstracted questioning: "What is borne amongst them?" … This question could apply to the separate poems of the entire sequence (with "born" a relevant mishearing in the context of Christmas). Here, as elsewhere, meaning comes tightly packed, yet still highly elusive. The clipped messages "broadcast" from the page like the coded wireless transmissions of a later and different negotiation between the two nations in Hill's own boyhood – "the Frankish gift … is carried over", REPEAT, "the Frankish gift … is carried over" – OVER AND OUT.

XXIV, as final instance, encodes Hill's idea of the artist as well as his vision of a once-and-future "Mercia". The hero is a mason (not architect or "auctor"): he is represented as having undertaken a pilgrimage to Compostela, from which he returns to ply his trade in West Mercia, "confusing warrior with lion, dragon-coils, tendrils of the stony vine" (128). The confusion – man, beast, monster and carved plant – is the confusion of all artifice and all attempts, too, to rationalise the apparent singularity of the human project – as history, philosophy or science. The mason "pesters" stone as mind pesters materiality. What is created is not Truth but a "moody testament". In the second verset Hill posits the characteristically postmodern question: "Where best to stand?" The poet seeks some perspective on the past – as Graham Swift in *Waterland*, A. S. Byatt in *Possession* or Peter Ackroyd in *English Music*[26] – but, like them, he finds the present modifies the past as the past can dominate the present. Adam "scrumps" (still a word for stealing fruit in the West Country) and a "cross Christ" (precocious punning) lives on to take him out of the infernal regions. The concluding Latin is referred in the notes to a musical piece by Olivier Messaien (postmodern connoisseur of bird-song – "clawing wings" – and the glories of organ music). So "Et expecto .... " constitutes a return of the spiritual repressed, the "Shadow of Spirit"[27] – an artistic recycling of Christian mystery beyond Marxist metanarrative and neo-Pragmatist "sophistry"[28] alike.

Geoffrey Hill's poetry, like Ginsberg's, is in the world but not of it: it would be misleading to term it "postmodernist" as the word is fashionably used. Nevertheless, it is postmodern in a double sense: it uses as its example and springboard the major writings of such modernists as Eliot, Pound and the later Yeats and it views the period of late modernity (that, for instance, of Charles Péguy) from a scanning position informed by Auschwitz, Hiroshima, ecological ravagement and the consumer society. It constitutes "historiographic metafiction", in the sense that Linda Hutcheon has used the catch-all phrase to denominate recent fiction, but it was achieved before most such fiction was written. It is *sui generis*, for Hill is an individualist whose quirky creations owe little to any *Zeitgeist*, ideology or pre-sumed "condition". However, in *Mercian Hymns* particularly, Hill has established a poetic means of advancing the causes of both "beauty" and "truth" by taking sceptical deconstruction to its grammatical limits – and somehow saving an overall implication, as by fire. His "hymns" home in on history like a smart-bomb lens – magnifying the targeted "ventilation duct" before impacting to brilliant effect. His work is unique, craggy and, in a sense, neo-Baroque. But it is not just a "product" of our times – it rather provides a print-out of our times as a recycling of past passions and problems.

Mercian Hymns constitutes a codic poetic model that could be productively modified in future Anglo/American writing. As a sequence, it is split up into a round number of discrete epiphanies. It is expressed in a prose that dares to speak its name – but is more tellingly poetic than most recent verse and accords with the preference of contemporary Linguistics in operating through a-syntactical expressive units rather than conforming to some Graeco-Roman grammatical template. Like Auden's later verse, it can replicate the techniques of advertisement rhetoric – to catch at truth rather than induce commercial or political compliance. In content, it insists on the present pressure of past existence, on the ultimate ambiguity of both and on the radical dependence of both (most materially so) on a grounding in seasonal, ecological wholeness. It offers an ironic, if empathetic, anatomisation of masculinist endeavour in which femininity ("my grandmother", XXV, 129, or "Gran", XXIX 133) is a somewhat etherial and nostalgic presence. It is both an evocative and a sceptical sequence where "authenticity" is, at best, a trenchant representation of "la recherche de temps perdu" – whether historical or personal. It is idiosyncratic, yet no less socially relevant for that. And for all its formidable exactitude of phrase, it offers a prosaic formulation which can open up the expression of postmodernity to poets of a newer generation. As the last stanza of *The Mystery* puts it "Take that for your example" (196).

Notes

1. Geoffrey Hill, *Collected Poems* (Penguin, 1985), pp. 15–16.
2. Jeremy Hooker cites "echoes of Yeats, Blake and Coleridge", all of which are demonstrable. See "For the Unfallen: a sounding", in *Geoffrey Hill: Essays on his Work*, ed. Peter Robinson (Open University Press, 1985), p. 24. The poem was first called: "Genesis: A Ballad of Christopher Smart"!
3. For a pleasingly informal, though expert, account of the place of the Genesis narratives within early Mesopotamian culture see John Romer, *Testament: The Bible and History*, Channel 4 Book (Michael O'Mara, 1988), pp. 15–63.
4. "Besides", "other" or "alternative" world. I have borrowed the phrase from Christian Miquel, *Critique de la Modernité: l'exil et le social* (Editions L'Harmattan, 1992). "La fonction profonde de ces 'outre mondes' ... c'est de permettre à l'imaginaire de rêver sa propre vie, en se projetant dans une autre dimension et en oubliant grâce à cela sa condition exilique" (p. 70). I translate this (roughly) as: "The important function of these 'other worlds' is to allow the imaginary to dream its own life, aspiring to another dimension and so becoming oblivious to its condition of exile." Miquel, versed in Nietzsche, Foucault, Deleuze and Guattari and Baudrillard, is committed to the authenticity of "exile" and chooses "an-archie" against the "somnifères" (sleeping-pills?) "de la modernité" (p. 117): he thus finally despises "outre mondes" (as indeed much else). Hill's irony allows the "hymns" to evade Miquel's postmodernist Diogenism just

as the French phrase helps codify the historical fantasia that the "hymns" represent.

5. Hill's own phrase which Martin Dodsworth uses both for "Mercian Hymns" and St John Perse's precedent poem *Anabase*. See Dodsworth in "Mercian Hymns: Offa, Charlemagne and Geoffrey Hill", *Geoffrey Hill*, ed. Robinson, p. 56.

6. Hill's title "Three Baroque Meditations" (pp. 89–91) seems implicitly to acknowledge the mannered sophistication of his verbal craft. A recent book on this aspect of postmodern art is Omar Calabrese, *Neo-Baroque: A Sign of the Times*, trans. Charles Lambert (Princeton University Press, 1992), reviewed by Roger Scruton in *The Times Literary Supplement*, 18 December 1992.

7. Philip Larkin, *The Whitsun Weddings* (Faber and Faber, 1964), pp. 45–6. My comparison is not intended to suggest an "influence" either way.

8. Cf. Jeremy Hooker: "But is it possible that Geoffrey Hill, ironist and sceptic, really believes in Judgement Day? It is possible; what is certain, however, is that the book is haunted by a strongly felt need for a measure of man's worth that is absolute and terrifying, outside all his lying and comforting systems of self-evaluation" (*Geoffrey Hill*, ed. Robinson, p. 23).

9. Linda Hutcheon's key theme in *A Poetics of Postmodernism* – and well-argued in terms of recent prose fiction. She defines "historiographic metafiction" as "[novels] which are both intensely self-reflexive and yet paradoxically lay claim to historical events and personages" (p. 5). This seems to apply quite exactly to "Mercian Hymns".

10. Pound's opposition in Canto VIII, lines 1–3. See Ezra Pound, *The Cantos* (Faber and Faber, 1986), p. 28.

11. Where the "chronotope" of many centuries finds specific articulation and "every meaning" has its "homecoming festival". See M. M. Bakhtin, *Speech Genres and Other Late Essays*, trans. Vern W. McGee, ed. Caryl Emerson and Michael Holquist (University of Texas Press, 1986), p. 170.

12. "Animals are divided into: (a) belonging to the Emperor, (b) embalmed, (c) tame, (d) sucking pigs, (e) sirens, (f) fabulous, (g) stray dogs, (h) included in the present classification, (i) frenzied … ", etc. Quoted in Alan Sheridan, *Michel Foucault: The Will to Truth* (Tavistock, 1980), p. 46.

13. Hill quoted by Henry Hart in "Early Poems: Journeys, Meditations and Elegies", *Geoffrey Hill*, ed. Robinson, p. 15.

14. Dorothy Whitelock, *The Beginning of English Society* (Penguin, 1956), p. 48.

15. *Sweet's Anglo-Saxon Reader: in Prose and Verse*, revised throughout by C. T. Onions, described as quoted, in the thirteenth edition (Clarendon Press, 1954), title page.

16. *Ibid.*, p. 170.

17. Ezra Pound, *The Cantos*, p. 3.

18. See Martin Dodsworth's quite thorough account in *Geoffrey Hill*, ed. Robinson, p. 53.

19.   In addition to Ong's *Orality and Literacy* see Elizabeth L. Eisenstein, *The Printing Revolution in Early Modern Europe* (Cambridge University Press, 1983).

20.   Last English words in the pre-Pisan *The Cantos*, LXXI, p. 421.

21.   Ezra Pound, *Selected Poems, 1908–1959* (Faber and Faber, 1981), p. 111.

22.   Vincent B. Sherry, Jr, "Geoffrey Hill" in *The Dictionary of Literary Biography*, vol. 40 (Bruccoli Clark, 1985), p. 208.

23.   See, for instance, Michael Rustin, *The Good Society and the Inner World: Psychoanalysis, Politics and Culture* (Verso, 1991) and Meg Harris Williams and Margot Waddell, *The Chamber of Maiden Thought: Literary Origins of the Psychoanalytic Model of the Mind* (Tavistock/Routledge, 1991).

24.   David Jones, *The Anathemata: Fragments of an Attempted Writing* (Faber and Faber, 1952).

25.   From "East Coker", T. S. Eliot, *The Complete Poems and Plays* (Faber and Faber, 1969), p. 178.

26.   Graham Swift, *Waterland* (Picador, 1984), A. S. Byatt, *Possession: a Romance* (Vintage, 1990), Peter Ackroyd, *English Music* (Hamish Hamilton, 1992).

27.   A conference with this title was held at King's College, Cambridge, in July 1990. The resulting book is *Shadow of Spirit: Postmodernism and Religion*, edited by Philippa Berry and Andrew Wernick (Routledge, 1992).

28.   See Christopher Norris, *What's Wrong with Postmodernism: Critical Theory and the Ends of Philosophy* (Harvester/Wheatsheaf, 1990), p. 130.

8

John Ashbery's "Wave"

The extraordinary free-verse meditation "A Wave" (1983) is the last *essai* in John Ashbery's *Selected Poems* of 1987.[1] The evocative title can be read as a cannily ambiguous try-on: it immediately suggests oceanic rhythmicality, but there are also implicit intimations of the "wave-theory"[2] of modern physics (key principle and metaphor for the "electric age") and, at least, an implication of gestural nonchalance which Stevie Smith had contrasted to "drowning"[3] and John Berryman acted out as farewell salute to an uncomprehending world (see above, Chapter 5). In contrast to the existential intensity of Smith's polarisation and Berryman's casual desperation, Ashbery's "Wave" represents a zone of apparently relaxed, postmodern hyperreality where experience is a constant renegotiation between a hypostasised "we" of communality and the environmental *simulacra* which surround and help define the contemporary human project. "A Wave" inscribes a cool, street-wise Heraclitianism where insubstantiality is almost sacralised as material being and the pragmatic present ("the ground on which a man and his wife could / Look at each other and laugh, remembering how love is to them", 331) is all that can be constituted. Ashbery's style represents postmodernity through a kind of linguistic *mimesis* of flux in its verbal fluidity, calculated vaguery and eclectic artificiality: in this it can fittingly be termed "postmodernist". Yet, whether "influence" is a factor or not, its moments of being and its peculiar affect have a notable precedent in the work of Virginia Woolf, who wrote about being "afloat upon … reality"[4] and suggested, even before beginning to pen her novel *The Waves*, that "on a summer's day waves collect, overbalance, and fall; and the world seems to be saying 'that is all' ".[5]

The first poem in the Ashbery collection posits observational analysis with reference to habitual enactment: "We see us as we truly behave" ("Two Scenes", 3). The poem links the metaphysical factitiousness of Wallace Stevens to the painterly idiosyncracy of New York Abstract Expressionism, yet the theme seems to be less visual space than processive time: the present tense verb is used as index of being-as-becoming; "comes", "strikes", "guides", "anoints". Although the poem's title suggests two different scenes, they seem to blur into one ongoing revelation of events in progress. The day is marked out from the machinery of "History" as a concatenation of "news" and "noise", impossible to demarcate in the "singular authority" of some metaphysical speculation or linear narrative; already there is established the Ashbery waywardness in setting slightly odd and incompatible terms in quizzical relationship (for example, "dry as poverty") and wringing out of the contrastiveness of different ranges of diction a wry and laconic music. At the end, some passing cadets are summoned out of nowhere to voice the omnipresence of a "schedule" never specified – "Wave" as regularity, fluidity and progressiveness, beyond any neo-Platonic fixity of Idea.

"The Instruction Manual", also from *Some Trees* (1956), is itself "instructive" since it polarises two experiential planes – that of present perception and that of dreamlike reverie – which are typically interfused as one "reality" (a kind of simulation realism) in the bizarre affectivity of Ashbery's mature work. As Marjorie Perloff has pointed out, in this poem the "reality – dream – reality structure ... is a simplified version of the 'greater romantic lyric' as Meyer Abrams and others have defined it".[6] The poem begins with the banal task of the manual writer in his city building, proceeds to elaborate a quite lengthy, Chirico-like "dream" of Guadalajara and finally returns to the manual as job in hand. However, where the poem differs strongly from romantic lyricism is in its deployment of laid-back, neomodernist irony. The whole piece, in fact, is less an exercise in flight from urban reality ("in city pent", as Wordsworth or Coleridge would term it) than a dry and sophisticated send-up of the travelogues, exotic advertisements and TV travel programmes of postmodernity. Different parts of the (imaginary) city are highlighted in technicolour detail through a drawling line which mocks the predictable "voice-over" as tellingly as Peter Sellers' skit "Bal-ham gateway to the South": – "Your public square, city, with its elaborate little bandstand!" (5) or "There is the poorer quarter, its homes a deep blue" (7). As in much of later Ashbery, the poetic diction and tone have so introjected the clichés and flattened-out rhythms of the programmed voice that the lines walk a tightrope between pastiche and banality. It builds to its conclusion with a preposterous resumé: "We have heard the music, tasted the drinks, and looked at colored houses" (8) – yet even here there is a kind of auditory music which reminds us of early Eliot as well as of Stevens or, say, Baudelaire. A typical Ashbery poem seems to inhabit naturally, as well as mimetically express, the self-reflexive and self-parodic experience of postmodernity as theoretically represented in Baudrillard's "On Seduction" and "Simulacra and Simulations"[7] or Deleuze and Guattari in "Capitalism and Schizophrenia".[8] Like Allen Ginsberg, Ashbery has been encapsulating, formulating and satirising the postmodern from the fifties onwards. A middle-career poem like "Decoy" (105–6) exemplifies his dead-pan (a word given transitive verbal form in the poem) and unsettlingly ironic method. It commences by citing (without quotation marks) the first proposition of the American Constitution, but by the second line the recital of "these truths" has been slyly applied to social "ostracism". Thereafter the poem invokes the mysterious interpenetration of capitalism, law, industrialism and "urban chaos" of the contemporary USA in a language which mocks by mimicry rather than "demystifies" by rational extrapolation. Indeed, while the lines identify a "descending scale of values", they also seem to satirise the chief oppositional description of the time, the Marxist narrative of the crisis and collapse of late capitalism: "the imminent lateness of the denouement that, advancing slowly, never arrives" (105). These words were written at least ten years before Fredric Jameson and Terry Eagleton were responding to the theorisation of the "postmodern condition" in terms of the same Marxist master narrative – "self-styled prophets of commercial disaster" both. To be sure, waves – in the sea at least – do eventually break, but Ashbery's "Wave" seems more like those electronic and magnetic waves that circulate endlessly within the "curves" of space (if that is quite what they do) and his contemporaneous "history" seems the same, "turning and wheeling aimlessly". As spatial reality is appearance so time here is flux, for all our "plotting itineraries". Thus, the poem seeks resolution in a simulation of "life, liberty and the pursuit of happiness" – a quite allegorical (and anonymous) man and woman, on a bed, "kicking out into the morning" (106).

Like Geoffrey Hill, Ashbery can invest prose with the exploratory particularity and rhythmic purpose of the poetic line – though Hill's versets are minimalist and Ashbery's prose poems elaborate a self-reflexive plenitude. The most spectacular instance of a prose poem by Ashbery is "The System" (127–64) from *Three Poems* (1972). This originally followed the poem "The New Spirit" written in the late sixties for Elliott Carter's *Concerto for Orchestra*, inscribing the particular mood felt in the USA during that era:

> Something is happening. The new casualness had been intro-
> ducing itself, casually of course, but suddenly its credentials lay
> everywhere ... as though the news had already broken out and
> was flooding the city and the whole country.[9]

"The System" contains its own form of urgency, its first words being "The system was breaking down" (127), yet its *via negativa* mystical gestures and its allusions to , say, Lazarus (157) and Pascal (129), as well as its half-references to the verse of T. S. Eliot,[10] suggest a grounding where "the news" is merely a contemporary instance of the individual's struggle with "whatever was, is, and must be" (150 and 155).[11]

The drift of the poem tends to modulate from a generalised "you" to a re-affirmatory "I" and it subtly combines Biblical "high style" ("Who has seen the wind?", 132) with ironic low style ("careers which will 'peak' after a while", 139). However, it seems to me unfruitful to regard Ashbery's method, as Keith Cohen has done, as a "dismantling of bourgeois discourse".[12] Cohen sets up his essay with a quotation from Roland Barthes: "Suppose that the intellectual's (or the writer's) historical function, today, is to maintain and emphasize the *decomposition* of bourgeois consciousness". That Ashbery habitually operates through irony (and frequently through parody and pastiche) is incontestable. But Barthes' type of European, neo-Marxist fashionability is precisely what answers to the poem's early critique of the "dominant party", wedded to the illusion of "the logical last step of history" (133). Terms such as "intellectual", "historical function", "decomposition" and "bourgeois" are put under erasure by all that the poem says – ("I'm speaking needless to say not of written history but the oral kind that goes on in you without your having to do anything about it", 128). What is at issue here is not a metadiscursive "historical function", with all its inauthentic presumption of access to true consciousness but the creative process through which the poet can weave a "Wave" of words to encode the historical and linguistic processes of contemporary America.

In fact, Ashbery's subject and style, here, are not as unprecedented as some admirers imply. Much of his manner (and towards the end, matter)[13] is reminiscent of Bernard's summing-up in Woolf's *The Waves*. Auden had been an early sponsor of Ashbery's work and it is most likely that the younger poet would have been aware of Caliban's penultimate (and parodic) peroration in "The Sea and the Mirror", which foreshadows much of the technique adopted in "The System". Further, the example of Samuel Beckett's turgidly self-reflexive (and neo-Pascalian) narrators seems akin to Ashbery's Americanised ironic reflections. Let us try conclusions:

> Immeasurably receptive, holding everything, trembling with fullness, yet clear, contained – so my being seems, now that desire urges it no more out and away; now that curiosity no longer dyes it a thousand colours.[14]

> Yet, at this very moment when we do at last see ourselves as we are, neither cosy nor playful, but swaying out on the ultimate wind-whipped cornice that overhangs the unabiding void – we have never stood anywhere else, – when our reasons are silenced by the heavy huge derision, – There is nothing to say.[15]

> No, life ends and no, there is nothing elsewhere, and no question now of ever finding again that white speck lost in whiteness, to see if they still lie still in the stress of that storm, or of a worse storm, or in the black dark for good, or the great whiteness unchanging, and if not what they are doing.[16]

> I know now that I am no longer waiting, and that the previous part of my life in which I thought I was waiting and therefore only half-alive was not waiting, although it was tinged with expectancy, but living under and into this reply, which has suddenly caused everything in my world to take on new meaning.
> ("The System", 159)

In each case, the sentences typically unwind in meditative, self-questioning subunits which conform to quasi-philosophical abstractions, suddenly enlivened by some surprise image and all teasing out, periphrastically, the meaning of being and the limits of communication. Ashbery's postmodernism, we might fairly comment, here establishes itself in dialogue with the more prosaic "voices" of modernism and neomodernism to question the "new spirit" of postmodernity.

I take it that this poem works through its overall stylistic posture and its moments of self-reflexive insight rather than in terms of any coherent "argument". It is not that the poem represents a merely parodic exercise in metaphysical depthlessness but that such genuine "Areopagite" depth as it succeeds in expressing is not susceptible to extrapolation as "explanation" or "analysis". The dominant posture is "as though" (but treated as a cupola between relative incompatibles rather than index or reinforcing instance) and so I read the text's neophilosophical distinctions – what "seemed" a "new point" (133), "an alternative way would be ... " (139) or "the second kind, the latent or dormant kind" (141) – as quasi-Beckettian instances of sceptical irony. As the poem has it: "forget also the concepts and archetypes that haunt you"(151). Just as Auden's Caliban is "Platonic" only in so far as he constitutes a Christianised mode of Socratic ignorance, looking for the "real Word", so Ashbery's filmic text posits "a question ... still waiting for the answer" (158), with only a wishful intimation of "a god come down to earth to instruct us in the ways of the other kingdom" (144). The meditative "stance" is in fact a postmodern point in time "moving forward continually" (141)) where the religious "return of the repressed" is a kind of back-projection to the insubstantial moving scene. The "Wave" here is as much a river as a sea movement (perhaps with *Huckleberry Finn* in mind), gliding through time (January to February and beyond), where "life's rolling river" (131), the "vast waving mass" (130), is proceeding towards some landing which always recedes. It is wasted time, we are told, that "sinks into the sea" (164). The anguish of the largely generalised persona concerns how to keep balance and take bearings as the "Wave" advances remorselessly, each instance unfolding its new demands. The radical apprehension of experiential flux, here, is familiar in terms of Heraclitus or Walter Pater or Henri Bergson (not to mention the turbulent shadows against which Platonic Forms assert themselves). The uniqueness resides in the contemporary language and scenarios and the American-pragmatic choice of protagonist (a kind of proto-Rorty), "the average, open-minded, intelligent person" (129) who despite time's "eddies", "shallows" and "rapids" (131), seeks to navigate through to "the pragmatic and kinetic future" (164).

In "Daffy Duck in Hollywood" (235–8), from *Houseboat Days* (1977), Ashbery's contrastive technique of radical pastiche is well exemplified. Evoking the original celluloid "Disney World", it

sardonically queries "what happened to creative evolution?" (236)
– Bergson's idealistic, if neo-Lamarckian, chronology of élan vital –
through a Mickey Mouse mélange of junk phrases both exotic and
banale:

> ... – a mint-condition can
> Of Rumford's Baking Powder, a celluloid earring, Speedy
> Gonzales, the latest from Helen Topping Miller's fertile
> Escritoire, a sheaf of suggestive pix on greige, deckle-edged
> Stock – ...
>
> (235)

This is knowing (even Camp?) New York appropriation-satire,
couched in sardonic, wrap-around free-verse lines which leave only
a space of ambiguous mediation ("between") to imply the absence
of a point of view. But then point of view suggests Perspective – in
the art history terms Ashbery was familiar with – already out-
moded by the time of post-Impressionism. The poem fully bears
out Clement Greenberg's notion of a "tradition of the new", except
that here tradition – that which is handed on – concerns not *avant-
gardism* but schlock and kitsch culture. Nevertheless, "Walt" no less
than, say, Jackson Pollock or Robert Rauschenberg, is impelled by
the irrationally futuristic forces of postmodernity in a vortex of flux,
simulation, dementia and demotic vulgarity that would have made
Wyndham Lewis turn in his grave.[17] This "allegory" constitutes a
series of cartoon-like speed-ups and metamorphoses: "clattering
through", "get me out of this one", "How will it end?", "even now",
etc. It is a Hollywood film world of narrative hyperreality which
will shortly permeate the "global village" as satellite TV twenty-
four hours a day mulch. The poem wryly concludes that we "have
our earnest where it chances on us" (238). Let us hope so, but what
kind of "earnest" and who, quite, are "we"?

"A Wave" (330–51) succeeds in marrying the meditational
irony of "The System" with the gaudy pastiche of "Daffy Duck in
Hollywood" to achieve what I take to be the most profound and
weirdly beautiful Anglo/American "long-poem" (twenty-one
pages) of the eighties. It constitutes, I suggest, the "Tintern Abbey"
of postmodernity. For it is concerned with time, human experience
("we") and the reality of "landscape" – here one that has been
socially constructed ("came to be as it is today") and constantly
variable: "all of a sudden the scene changes" (330). It is an

inherently conurban and scheduled realm where Nature seems the exception, reached for – if only as counter-scene – through evocations of hill, plant life, shore or sky. Poetic meditation is here sprung from the natural habitat of Westernisation:

> ... There was the quiet time
> In the supermarket, and the pieces
> Of other people's lives as they sashayed or tramped past ...
>
> (334)

At the same time, such a translocal "universality" of experience entails its own inevitable global dimension: "The complications of our planet, its climate, its sonatinas / And stories" (348). Buildings, corridors, rooms and walls predominate – wave-like themselves in their temporary appearance of permanence – and out of such phenomena and the "inferior religions"[18] of variegated human behaviour played out in the midst of them, are evinced the metaphysical queryings, the verbal enactions and retractions of this ultra-cool, supremely sceptical, yet still communalist rehearsal of the "still, sad music of humanity".[19]

As Wordsworth's Tintern Abbey "Lines" constitute a triumph of achieved tone to articulate the bridge between eighteenth and nineteenth century sensibilities, so Ashbery's "A Wave" triumphantly constructs a tone to express the contrastive marvels and banalities of postmodern experience. Wordsworth redeployed Miltonic cadences to utter bardic solemnity, in ordered verbal grandeur:

> ... And I have felt
> A presence that disturbs me with the joy
> Of elevated thoughts; a sense sublime
> Of something far more deeply interfused ...
> A motion and a spirit, that impels
> All thinking things, all objects of all thought,
> And rolls through all things.
>
> (164)

Ashbery redeploys the modernist "free" line to speak the puzzled quizzicalities of a 1980s New York Leopold Bloom:

... One is almost content
To be with people then, to read their names and summon
Greetings and speculation, or even nonsense syllables and
Diagrams from those who appear so brilliantly at ease
In the atmosphere we made by getting rid of most amenities
In the interests of a bare, strictly patterned life ...

(338)

The clichés, oddities of diction and periphrastic elongations are all part of the expressive success, for "speculation" in the represented world can only be in terms of the excesses, odd felicities and deficiences of American English as socially given at the time. This is not to "refine the dialect of the tribe": there is no tribe, only a human melting-pot; no consistent "dialect", rather a broad argot shot through with abstract approximations and urban–oral formulae ("be with people", "at ease", "In the interests of", etc.).

Yet there is an ("early") Eliotic cautiousness ("almost", "or even") and insidious irony which raise the lines from banality to affective poetry. The voice can be heard as androgynous (one could imagine Laurie Anderson intoning the above lines) and close to the discourse of androids – in both respects it is compellingly post-modern. And the "wrap-around" line ("enjambement" seems old-world euphemism in this context) replicates contemporary speech rhythms from space-ship bulletins to political "releases", from airport announcements to autocue news. Ashbery's meditative dance with words is (almost hypnotically) made out of the language of his time, yet codified as a mode of apprehension and coping:

Enough to know that I shall have answered for myself soon,
Be led away for further questioning and later returned
To the amazingly quiet room in which all my life has been spent.

(351)

The laconic, laid-back voice (Humphrey Bogart, Paul Newman, Clint Eastwood) should not be snobbishly discounted as a vehicle of significance (if not "seriousness").[20] For this speaking style represents a transatlantic expressive norm in a world where Platonism is dead, but its shadow lives on to haunt the minds of the less-deceived. And for all its banalities, it is capable of both directness and subtlety: "It would be cockier to ask of heaven just what is this present / Of an old dishpan you bestowed on me?" (349). "Dishpan" may be simply dishpan, but "present" combines the notion of bestowal with that of phenomenological mystery – *Dasein, durée,* Real Presence. It is through the continuous blend of street drawl and metaphysical querying that Ashbery's voice achieves its unsettling affectivity.

Yet for all the apparent idiosyncrasy of the poem's tone, Ashbery's commendable project is to establish a communal mode of expression – a stylistics of "we" – where "the average person" (331) can be represented in postmodern verse. The "Wave" is represented as generally shared experience: "the way things have of enfolding / When your attention is distracted for a moment"[21] (345). Such experience is characterised as a range of surprise epiphanies or puzzles unsettling the behavioural norm, which is continuously described in terms of routines: "business as usual", "ever-repeated gestures", "system", "game", "phase", "route", "machinery", "rounds", "series", "game plan". If this construction of background habituality reminds us of the satirical vision of Wyndham Lewis[22] as transmuted into the unremitting symmetry of Beckett's low-life clowns, the surreal metamorphoses of "scene", the spectral emanations of beauty or poignance, the Baroque elaborations of idea strike an original dissonance – authentic articulation of a postmodernity where wonderment and puzzlement, as well as routine, are part of the common lot rather than the property of the privileged artist. The "honest / Citizens" (330 – the line-break creating its own ironic distance) are at the centre of this rambling peroration and their "musings" which are grist to the mill of Ashbery's Teflon muse.

This helps to explain the dream-like collocation of geographical *topoi,* the varied domestic interiors, the casual mélange of popular song and high instance ("an English horn", 342) which makes up the whole. Ashbery's "we" is a variable construct, *engagé* in its bewildered promotion of a solidarity where "situating the self" and "identity and modernity"[23] are common issues in the age of postmodernity. Hence, the whole poem consists of a broken, spiralling speculation, full of surprise revelations as well as "visions and revisions", concerning the "limited set of reflections we were given at the beginning" (350). If "we" constitutes a "rainbow coalition", it remains a rainbow essential to sanity when "Wave" evokes the memory of the pre-Flood modernists ("après moi ... "). For all the likely restrictedness of his audience, Ashbery's vision, like Whitman's, is essentially democratic. It is a postmodern poeticisation of "Here Comes Everybody".[24]

The communal experience of postmodernity is hypostasised in one part of the poem as a kind of mental *tsunami*:

> ... swamped
> As though by a giant wave that picks itself up
> Out of a calm sea and retreats again into nowhere ... .
>
> (343)

Where "The System" is peculiarly riverine, "A Wave" is essentially oceanic: it concerns global (and aerial) rhythmic fluidity as it "passes through" the human "system" (332). Yet although the possibility of tidal-wave catastrophe is postulated, leaving only a "remnant", the wave motion in the poem as a whole is less dramatic, gentler and more insidiously insistent, expressed in progressive typographical blocks of lines, some long, some shorter, which break into the reader's consciousness like the breakers and ripples of an average incoming tide. Here tone, line and sectional length all work together to achieve a casual, pervasive rhythmicality – like the "leaden waves" of Virginia Woolf's Big Ben in *Mrs Dalloway*. So two models of the postmodern are postulated: the hypothetical ("as though") "Wave" of revolutionary devastation and the rhetorically mimicked "Wave" of slow attrition and readjustment, line by line, sentence after sentence, section following section to the end. However, the latter model constitutes the norm. In fact, the poem overall inscribes the postmodern situation as a pulsive series of insubstantial manifestations, which human mentality makes sense of as best it can, with an undertone of possible apocalypse threatening quite drastic purgation. For all Ashbery's artifice, this is a wholly recognisable world – as the poem puts it simply, "our home".

Ashbery enthusiasts are wont to praise his cunning linguistic mediation: "the illumination of life turned into language and language turned into life".[25] In "A Wave" the poet offers his own striking metaphor as a new form of the "Mystic Writing Pad":[26] "and we sit down to the table again / Noting the grain of the wood this time and how it pushes through / The pad we are writing on and becomes part of what is written" (335). Earlier the poem had favoured words as "a density / Of strutted opinion doomed to wilt in oblivion" (331). Both suggestions help towards formulating the peculiar opaqueness and self-referentiality of Ashbery's writing, which nevertheless builds out of traces a "parallel world" which in all important particulars seems almost identical with our own – itself under the constant, immanent erasure of "oblivion". As elsewhere, the style can naturally incorporate "quotations" to thicken and complicate the effect – *"my mindless, oh"* (330) or on page 347, an extended passage in quotation marks which sounds like part of a Beckett narrative, replete with a reference to Zeno's Paradox. In a similar fashion, the language reaches out and away from its metaphysical core to embrace oral oddities – "chroniquers", "the blahs", "goofing off", *"frei aber einsam"* – which both replicate the historical, additive rapacity of the English language and give a wry exoticism to the whole, quite as distinctive as that in Wallace Stevens.

The base-line remains a casual "corporate" monologue, a soliloquy *pour nous* – full of clichés, stray abstractions and suddenly flamboyant images, like the narrative of some philosophical Philip Marlowe sleuthing for some truth of things that never emerges. There remains the pragmatic, American reverence for "the thing / ... there in all its interested variegatedness", but even this William Carlos Williams-style pursuit becomes dissolved into quasi-Eliotic scepticism: "doubts about how it / Actually was" (340). For in "A Wave" language tries to pull reality into the poem just as it is, while at the same time the identical language constantly avers that this is not really possible – or that, at this moment of meditative expression, both reality and linguistic trope have suddenly changed. This is Ashbery's "supreme fiction": a postmodern philosophy of "as though". And at its conclusion, "contingency, irony and solidarity"[27] remain in uneasy conjunction as caution and solace: "We'll / Stay in touch. So they have it, all the time. But all was strange" (351).

One can scarcely "sum up" John Ashbery's brand of poetic postmodernism – the arithmetic simply does not exist. Nor, I think, is it necessary to: the poems speak for themselves, as they also speak for the condition of postmodernity. However, one can insist that the case of Ashbery proves fairly conclusively that the postmodern aesthetic cannot be merely dismissed as promiscuously eclectic, inherently parasitic or incorrigibly depthless. As Harold Bloom has suggested, Ashbery "seems most himself when most ruefully and intensely Transcendental".[28] Bloom goes on to qualify

American Transcendentalism (both "the Old" and "the New") as a species of "visionary skepticism" (9). This makes particular sense in terms of poems like "Two Scenes", "The System" and "A Wave". In his more radically parodic performances, the poet can lampoon the American eagle as "Tweetie-Pie" quite as effectively as anyone – not an unimportant role when a recent President could describe the leader of an independent nation (whose Capital US planes bombed) as "loony-toons". However, just as, States-side, the poet must appear as the evident successor of Wallace Stevens, so in the international arena of literature written in English he represents the postmodernist poet par excellence. And in both these frames, it is Ashbery's ability to incorporate schmaltz, quotationality and cultural heterogeneity into a quasi-religious , poetic search (and Recherche) which qualifies him as the laureate of the hyperreal.

To stamp his achievement with such a label is intended as a compliment. It is not a description which would commend his texts to neo-Platonists, Logical Positivists or vulgar Marxists. But it is in common agreement with Douglas Crase's view of "The Prophetic Ashbery".[29] For his poetry, from its inception in the early fifties, has anticipated and charted the postmodern terrain which has far more recently been staked out by social theorists such as Jean-François Lyotard, Jean Baudrillard, Richard Rorty, Zygmunt Bauman and Anthony Giddens, not to mention the cloud of witnesses who follow in their train. The one thinker who roughly kept abreast of what both Ashbery and Ginsberg, in their different ways, were once saying about the Western world was Marshall McLuhan. For Ashbery's work has always been specifically a production of the "electric age" – where enlightenment is a function of lightning activity between interactive poles, rhetoric must always retain both ironic and iconic awareness and poetry itself must assume a role not as "legislator" (for there is no ultimate legitimisation) but as the "antennae" of "what is, was and must be" where "nothing is permanent" (145). "A Wave" impelled Ashbery's achievement into the eighties, when theorists and critics were finally prepared to confront the presuggested realities. His postmodern poetry was quite widely dubbed postmodernist – alongside, say Bofill's architecture or Pynchon's fiction. Yet he had been there before and prepared the way. His companionable irony, historical referentiality ("Self-Portrait in a Convex Mirror"), street-wise, linguistic levelling and painterly manipulation of aesthetic surface to imply a metaphysical implication were long in the making – and, hence, truly *avant-garde* for the Cultural Studies brigade who now contest all the visible institutional ground. Ashbery has given us a metaphor and icon which can accommodate both high and low cultures, both male and female production – the "Wave": postmodern simulacrum of our time, both visual and auditory encoding of what is past and passing and to come.

Notes

1. John Ashbery, *Selected Poems* (Paladin/Grafton Books, 1987).
2. Gillian Beer gave an excellent lecture on "Wave Theory and Modern Literature" at the first ESSE conference, University of East Anglia, September 1991.
3. "Not Waving But Drowning", Stevie Smith, *Selected Poems* (Penguin, 1982), p. 167.
4. Virginia Woolf, *Moments of Being: Unpublished Autobiographical Writing*, ed. Jeanne Schulkind (Grafton, 1989), p. 156.
5. Virginia Woolf, *Mrs Dalloway* (Vantage Edition, Hogarth Press, 1992), p. 33.
6. See Marjorie Perloff, "'Fragments of a Buried Life': John Ashbery's Dream Songs", in *Beyond Amazement: New Essays on John Ashbery*, ed. David Lehman (Cornell University Press, 1980), p. 75.
7. In Baudrillard, *Selected Writings*, pp. 149–65 and 166–84.
8. Gilles Deleuze and Felix Guattari, *Anti-Oedipus: Capitalism and Schizophrenia*, trans. Robert Hurley, Mark Seem and Helen R. Lang (Athlone Press, 1990).
9. John Ashbery, *Three Poems* (Viking, 1972), p. 45.
10. For example, "duration of its unique instant", p. 144; "the very place you set out from", p. 153.
11. Cf. "Of what is past, or passing, or to come", last line of "Sailing to Byzantium", W. B. Yeats, *Collected Poems* (Macmillan, 1967), p. 218.
12. Keith Cohen, "Ashbery's Dismantling of Bourgeois Discourse", in Lehman's *Beyond Amazement*, pp. 128–49.
13. Especially with respect to the self-interrogation of the first person subject as opposed to the projected "you".
14. Virginia Woolf, *The Waves* (Penguin, 1951), p. 250.
15. "The Sea and the Mirror", W. H. Auden, *Selected Poems*, p. 173.
16. Samuel Beckett, "Imagination Dead Imagine", *No's Knife: Collected Shorter Prose 1945–1966* (Calder and Boyars, 1975), p. 164.
17. Cf. "For in [Lewis's] denunciation of a style he associated with jazz, women (Stein, Loos), Jewish thinkers (Bergson, Einstein), 'dementia' and children's talk, we see a complex Nietzschean paradigm of the discourse of the slave impinging on the domain of the master – western man" (Dennis Brown, *Intertextual Dynamics*, pp. 128–9). For

an account of his views, especially with respect to the style and example of *Ulysses*, see my account of Lewis's work throughout. "Daffy Duck" corresponds approximately to the last, ironic words of Lewis's *The Apes of God* (1930): "Whoddlah DOOOO!"

18. Wyndham Lewis's phrase for inauthentic, automatic behaviour. See Wyndham Lewis, "Inferior Religions", *The Complete Wild Body*, edited by Bernard Lafourcade (Black Sparrow Press, 1982), pp. 315–19. This essay was first published in *The Little Review*, September 1917, through the good offices of Ezra Pound.

19. From "Lines: Composed a Few Miles Above Tintern Abbey, on Revisiting the Banks of the Wye during a Tour, July 13, 1798", William Wordsworth, *Poetical Works* (Oxford University Press, 1974), p. 164.

20. See my remarks regarding Allen Ginsberg (see Chapter 3).

21. Cf. "[History] gives when our attention is distracted", T. S. Eliot, "Gerontion", *Collected Poems and Plays*, p. 38.

22. See note 18 above.

23. Cf. Seyla Benhabib, *Situating the Self* and Lash and Friedman (eds), *Modernity and Identity*. For full references see Index and above.

24. "H C E", central character in James Joyce's *Finnegans Wake*.

25. Quoted by Richard Howard, *John Ashbery*, ed. Harold Bloom (Chelsea House, 1985), p. 17.

26. See Freud's comments on the "Mystic Writing Pad" and Derrida's comments on it in Jacques Derrida, "Freud and the Scene of Writing" in *Writing and Difference*, trans. with an introduction and additional notes by Alan Bass (Routledge & Kegan Paul, 1981), p. 226.

27. Cf. Richard Rorty, *Contingency, Irony and Solidarity*. For full reference see Index and above.

28. In *John Ashbery*, ed. Bloom, p. 8.

29. Douglas Crase, "The Prophetic Ashbery", *Beyond Amazement*, ed. Lehman, pp. 30–65.

9

R. S. Thomas's "Amen"

R. S. Thomas's 1986 collection, *Experimenting with an Amen*,[1] begins with the intriguing word "and"; the poem "Formula" commences "And for the soul / in its bone tent ... " (1). If the latter phrase reminds us of Sylvia Plath's valedictory "hood of bone",[2] the first word evokes the overall struggle of Thomas's career to date – the expression of the physical and spiritual bleakness of rural Wales, the search for a valid language to enable the "speech" of the present and the wrestling with the "spectre of spirit"[3] which haunts the money-machine world of postmodernity. The collection, as the poem, constitutes a late (if not last)[4] addendum to and recapitulation of all that Thomas's unique parish placement and vision has had to say about where we all are now. The poem tentatively posits the terrors of nuclear winter, inexpressible in the "benumbed" words of an exclusionary, scientistic discourse where "$E=mc^2$" is meaningful yet lethal and the term "soul", for instance, must play off a marginalised language game to attain any resonance in a "half-mast" realm of equations and Death Instinct. This short poem constitutes one kind of epitaph for humankind in a single, halting eight-line sentence. It is, itself, a formulaic, verbal code defining "Beyond the Limits"[5] in a scenario that exploits war game ultimate descriptions, yet is also relevant in terms of computer predictions of peace-time technological "over-shoot" as the "North" zone: "insatiate cormorant, / Consuming means, soon preys upon itself".[6]

A. E. Dyson has suggested[7] that Thomas's poetic career attained a new dimension and importance with the publication of *H'm* in 1972; I agree with this.[8] The first poem in this volume is "Once" – a personalised creation fable, almost certainly written in response to Ted Hughes' *Crow* collection, which, in turn, may well have had Geoffrey Hill's striking poem "Genesis" in mind and perhaps also George Macbeth's "Owl".[9] "Once" links the origin of man and woman to the advent of the "Machine" – Thomas's catch-all term for the economic-industrial complex at the motor heart of both modernity and postmodernity. The poem constitutes a contemporary myth which links evolutionary theory with process theology and gives an admonitory side glance at T. S. Eliot's "Fire Sermon" in the key poetic text of modernism. The "Phenomenon of Man"[10] is here elaborated as an allegory of postmodern awareness where "forms hungry for birth" characterise both past physical development and future mind constantly on the move. Yet the distinctiveness of Thomas's contribution to postmodern art in general is evident in his grounding of process (and the poem) in God, who "looked" and set the whole train of being in motion. God is also represented as speaking – though the voice induces only fear in the contemporary Adam. This figure is given his Eve ("I took your hand") and they venture out to test their destiny; yet the worth of human sexual relationship (and progeny) is called into question by the imminence of mechanistic technology. This also casts doubt on the meaning of nature and the purpose of the God said to have initiated the human journey. It is, in particular, this dichotomy between the ways of God and the means and meanings of technologised science which Thomas's later poetry will turn to again and again, "experimenting" with the possibility of an "Amen" on behalf of incarnate postmodernity – which the poet typically views with distaste and mistrust.

In Thomas's later poetry, bone and stone are almost synonymous: both designate a bleak yet survivalist (sometimes flowering) natural realm which is "sicklied o'er" by the shadow of contemporary consciousness – where the "white coats" of scientists preside over "the Last Sacrament of the species" ("Ritual", 28). The phenomenon of physical survival had been an early theme of the poet's work: the figure of Iago Prytherch[11] had embodied it, while a striking line in "Song at the Year's Turning" – "You cannot stanch the bright menstrual blood"[12] – inscribed a "covenant" of natural process, seasonal rhythmicality and random promise of new life within the stark conditions of existence. *Experimenting with an Amen* is a book of old age where the "bone/ladder" predominates, as human grounding in the mineral world, but the issue becomes increasingly the effects of mind on the material realm and the possibility of sustaining survival when technology (inevitably) encounters negative feedback to its own incursions and to its inherent complicity with a malign economic system:

> I see the blinds
> going down in Europe, over the

whole world: the rich with everything to
sell, the poor with nothing to buy it with.

("The Window", 36)

Within such a "failed culture" ("Song", 27), the neo-Darwinian
imperative to survive, compete and reproduce one's kind scarcely
transcends such a "re-assembling of the species" ("Bequest", 43).

However, Thomas's unique poetic contribution is to combine a
critique of triumphalist scientism with a deconstruction of traditional theological metanarrative. Granted that his poetic career
began in the heyday of fifties' British positivism, it is not surprising
that Thomas found Christian belief, rather than the master narratives of "Gutenberg"[13] philosophising, under attack and, hence, in
need of redefinition. Almost instinctively, he examines the situation
of faith not in terms of master texts (Augustine or Tillich on the one
hand, Hume or Ayer on the other) but in terms of "petits récits" –
epiphanies recounting the piety of an agricultural labourer, the
devotion and anguish of a mother or the vision and honest doubts
of a parish priest. Postmodern *avant la lettre*, Thomas's verse has
consistently explored the realities of "common practice and particularity".[14] *Experimenting with an Amen* continues this process. It is
fully in line with recent theological understandings of belief as
expressed in David F. Ford's *The Modern Theologians*:

> Postmodern concepts of rationality and knowledge emphasise
> historical and cultural variability, fallibility, the impossibility of
> getting beyond language to "reality", the fragmentary and
> particular nature of all understanding, the pervasive corruption
> of knowledge by power and domination, and the need for a
> pragmatic approach to the whole matter.
>
> (292)

The collection also reinforces Jürgen Moltmann's perception in
Theology Today[15] that "Theology must accept the changed circumstances of the world in order to change these in its turn towards
peace, justice and the life of creation." Thomas's poetry is insistently self-reflexive in the face of both modern and postmodern
realities; it constantly queries its own aspirations and language-
base – but it also operates dialogically to challenge the new,
unaccountable structures at work:

> ... What anthem have our computers
> to insert into the vacuum caused
> by the break in transmission
> of the song upon Patmos?
>
> ("Reply", 65)

D. Z. Phillips has written persuasively and at length about the *Deus absconditus* ("hidden God")[16] in Thomas's *oeuvre*. However, the argument in his book tends to speak back to the monological discriminations of philosophical modernity rather than anticipate the polyglot symposia of interdisciplinary postmodernity. In fact, his book was published in the same year as *Experimenting with an Amen* and, hence, does not address the newer collection. However, the idea of assessing Thomas's work not in terms of "Welsh Poetry" but as international poeticisation of the contemporary *via negativa* is a good one and his book provides a basis for understanding the poet's later work. Phillips quotes to good effect Thomas's 1976 Eisteddford lecture where the poet evokes "Abercuawg", the legendary community where "the cuckoos sing": it is not to be found, yet there is "a way of getting to know better, through its absence, the nature of the place we are looking for". By analogy, this is like "man's condition". For he "is always about to comprehend God; but insofar as he is a creature and finite, he will never succeed".[17] This is how Divinity is expressed in the poem "Via Negativa":

> ... God is that great absence
> In our lives ...
> > where we go
> Seeking ... .
>
> (*Later Poems*, 23)

In "Cones" (*Experimenting*, 3), borrowing from T. S. Eliot, this "absence" is represented as "the still/centre". Such a perception cannot be elaborated satisfactorily in narrative at all – let alone "explained" and rationalised in a master text. The *Deus absconditus* of later R. S. Thomas comes coded in short, pungent lyrics where the information systems of postmodern materiality are most in evidence.

Thomas's mature work has given a high profile to the notion of "language games". In particular, his verse has laboured to free a truly human speech from the dominating discourses of materialism: "It addressed / objects, preferred its vocabulary / to their own" ("Brother", *Later Poems*", 204). This "brother" ends up loosing missiles out of gravity's reach to pollute space itself. What the poet seeks to counter is the consolidation of scientific discourse as Will-to-Power within a language war considerably older than the phenomenon of logical positivism in his early career. Here, for instance, is T. H. Huxley in a lecture, "On the Physical Basis of Life", originally delivered in Edinburgh in 1868:

> with a view to the progress of science ... materialistic language is in every way to be preferred. For it connects thought with the other phenomena of the universe, and suggests inquiry into the nature of those physical conditions, or concomitants of thought, which are more or less accessible to us, and a knowledge of which may, in future, help us to exercise the same kind of control over the world of thought, as we already possess in respect of the material world; whereas, the alternative, or spiritualistic terminology is utterly barren, and leads to nothing but obscurity and confusion of ideas.[18]

It is not to invalidate the conventions of scientific communication to resist their incursion into every aspect of human speech and writing – especially since terms such as "progress of science", "control over ... the material world" and "barren" (as a description of spirituality) have an ironic ring in the ecologically sensitive nineties. Thomas's poetry dialogically incorporates the terms of scientistic philosophy but does so in order to highlight what it has excluded and repressed (for any discursive formation works by promoting some terms and *excising* or marginalising others) and to sponsor, at once, both a more spiritualistic and a more environmentally benign language. "Prayer", the last poem in *Later Poems* (214) concludes with the words:

> ... the tree of poetry
> that is eternity wearing
> the green leaves of time.

In *Experimenting with an Amen*, "benumbed language" (1) is still set against the speech of the striving soul. As a bird may sing to us of God ("Message", 56) so the poet's role is to teach "flight's/true purpose" ("A Poet", 6). This may concern both nourishing the "green/twig" ("This One", 58) of living speech and recycling the language forms of the past: in "A Country" (2) the poet is one who "repairs" names and decorates his buttonhole with the past at the wedding of new generations to their future. In keeping with his *via negativa* vision, Thomas can use the very inability of technological language to speak to and of our inner humanity as an indication that other forms of communication are essential, however, he also adopts a positive discursive policy which I have described elsewhere: "he improvises, deconstructs, straddles sentence across line and detonates his sudden surprise images".[19] As in "Calling" (31) the poet seeks "the code" to dial "collect-call" to God, so his own verse attempts to construct a linguistic encoding of the dialectic between man and the divine: "the spinning / of two minds, the one on the other" ("Cones", 3).

Yet Thomas's "Amen" is as much a benediction on the stark, yet sometimes epiphanic, terrain of human experience as it is the acknowledgement of an eternal dimension which might inform it. He speaks from an acknowledged "margin" – contemporary rural Wales – yet this specified space–time "zone" can be read off as typical of present basic needs and desires. A poem like "The Unvanquished" expresses the dignity of all breadline experience, irrespective of specific geography: "When they died, it / was bravely" (30). If the oppressed, most particularly, cannot choose the nature of their sufferings, each individual retains human freedom in terms of the "response". The lives of the poet's neighbouring farmers are far more representative of global realities, even in the nineties, than the life-styles of a New York poet or a Parisian *philosophe*. The "Machine" impinges on them, as it does on almost everyone, yet the domain of the hyperreal (with or without television) is here localised as all-too realistic "phlegm" and "rain-hammered rafters". The average Ieuan Morgan ("Aim", 64) inhabits a world not substantially transformed out of its component elements of "animal, vegetable, mineral". This is as true of "postmodern" Newfoundland, Kazakhstan, Alabama or Somalia as it is of Thomas's own keenly observed turf. The "Amen" applies to what is lived as well as to the newer reaches of what can be known or sponsored. And as the last poem in the volume tells us about the subtle gimmicks of a technological age, "we can do without them" (70): however painful that might now prove to be – Amen to that.

There is the "sense of an ending"[20] about *Experimenting with an Amen*. In this the volume also projects the "Poetry of Postmodernity" towards the mythic impact point of the Year 2000 and the third millennium. Certainly, Thomas interrogates both the relevant "exigencies" and the "limitations" of our unique temporal placement in the poem "AD 2000" (25). Here W. B. Yeats's portentous gyres are evoked in conscious quotationality to preside over the important question:

> What power shall minister to us
> at the closure of the century,
> of the millennia?

In the manner of Dietrich Bonhoeffer, humankind is here seen to have "come of age". Delivered from the tyranny of mere manual labour ("the hand"), our species is confronted by the terms of freedom – an achieved, clear-eyed consciousness of consciousness, which is the self-realisation of materiality bought at the price of *angst*. Divinity, represented as "Janus-faced" (God/Devil?), has become "eclipsed" by modern mentality – the planetary bulk of our accumulated awareness. Yet there remains still a "halo", the glow of presence effected by absence. The poem quite typically ends on a question. Does contemporary mind retain a relevant numinosity on account of this residual "radiation" and is this enough to provide grounds for affirmation and a continued reverence?

Earlier in the volume, "Cones" (3) appears to assume a positive response to such questioning – God is a term boldly readopted in the pursuit of understanding. Indeed, this is still a God of design, although that is described rather than argued for: a teleological principle made self-evident in terms of leaf, shell and star. A reciprocity is established between man's investigative consciousness and the purposive consciousness of God: this is not unlike Anselm's ontological argument where the grandeur of the Divine Idea guarantees its validity for the postulating human mind. Again utilising Yeats's cosmogony, Thomas uses its dynamic to redefine the conclusion to Eliot's *Four Quartets* – we do not "arrive" at the place we started from but revisit it "from a distance", in a dream-like state of recognition. Thomas, like Eliot here, recognises the "ruins" of false beginnings and misrecognitions yet inscribes an almost inevitable spiralling relationship between divine and human consciousness. Like John Ashbery, he co-opts a collective human "we" to represent contemporary awareness. However, the aim is not epistemological but ontological: "we" seek not God's "reflections" but his "presence" at the still centre. The divine "zone" is characterised by love and it is transmitted as such, as a dialogical interchange of "frequencies". The ideas in the poem are familiar: Thomas is not a representative of modernity – starting an investigation inductively, *ab initio* and, thus, "Voyaging through strange seas of thought, alone";[21] he is spokesperson for postmodernity, accepting the findings of contemporary mathematical–scientific intelligence but sifting these through a recycling of Platonic and Dantesque tropes and through a self-conscious dialogue with the master poets of modernism, Yeats and Eliot. In this, the poem exercises a human form of love in reciprocity with the divine principle: the "spinning" of minds in productive conjunction.

In "Apostrophe" (9) the figure of axial love retains its conclusory power. *Chambers English Dictionary* refines the title word in terms of a "sudden turning away from the ordinary course of a speech to address a person or object present or absent".[22] In the poem there is a person ("he") who is, in a sense, "present" and the poetic subject ("I") speaks back to his perceptions of human improvisation ("they"). In fact, the poem may well constitute a "Dialogue of Self and Soul".[23] For the initial sentiments, attributed to third-person opinion, are familiar in Thomas's work from at least *Later Poems* onwards. They amount to a cumulative critique of modern human self-deception and squandering of natural resources. The metanarrative of modernity as ongoing, linear "ascent", accompanied by cumulative empirical discovery, is seen as wrong from the start – "on the wrong track". In fact, the whole notion of "track" is here placed under critical erasure. Residual ignorance and the consolations of the changing "view" are alike subordinated to the compulsion of Will to Truth: astronomical observation, evolutionary theory and space-programmes are alike indicted as deviations from wisdom, effecting instability and at the expense of planetary environmental wealth. The exploratory metaphor at the heart of such hectic activity is rebuked in the shorter second section of the poem. "There are no journeys", the poet boldly declares. This is, of course, on the surface of the statement untrue: the world is obsessed by journeying, getting somewhere, moving on again. Yet the word "journey" itself helps point toward the critique which Thomas is making, for, etymologically, it denotes merely the travel that can be accomplished in one day ("journée"), so that spatial exploration is conflated back into the limitations of biological temporality and these in turn raise the question of meaningful activity and productive being. In "every generation", the poet suggests, what matters is the relation of humanity to the axis of *agape* and wisdom resides in contemplating this in stillness. Once more, the model of majestic "turning" is sponsored in place of the Western mania for advance.

"Destinations" (14) is a poem with a similar dialogical component, but here the "they" of the "formless company" and the "I" of the poetic subject can at least be hypothesised as "we" and "travelling" can be hypostatised – in a contrastive "petit récit" – as a journey towards "light". Here the vision is similar to that of Teilhard de Chardin where civilisation, science and consciousness are similarly engaged in a trajectory away from the "bone's wisdom" towards the cosmic self-realisation of final illumination. The poem plays off the representations of spiralling discovery in both Eliot's "Journey of the Magi" and his *Four Quartets*.[24] There are not only journeys; there is also an ongoing human movement which, however distracted by the voices of ignorance and reaction, is towards the "ethereal in us". There is both a "Martian" and a cosmic component to "Destinations" which provides a Science Fiction feel ("remote/star") to this rewriting of evolutionary causality as a teleological process toward the consummation of both materiality and aspiring idealism. Again, *agape* is the quality which makes a new "zone" possible – though God is not inscribed as a direct player in this game of directions. Rather it is human intelligence and awareness that bring to a cautiously optimistic conclusion the dialogue between being and nothingness, darkness and lighting:

> ... the brightness over
> an interior horizon, which is science
> transfiguring itself in love's mirror.

The same theme is taken up in "Strands" (32), though its last sentence questions, rather than offers an answer. The poem expresses the difficulty of human experience in terms of three contrastive motivations and modes of behaviour – the regressive ("uterine"), the masochistically projective ("come/to be weighed") and the rationally exploratory ("nature, mechanism, evolution"). The last is extrapolated in terms evocative of both the imaginative breakthroughs of Lascaux or Altamira and Plato's powerful figure of the cave of awareness – now lit up by an electricity which can also search "beyond the galaxies". However, scientific discovery is posited here in possible relation to an ultimate nothingness, a "hole" dug by the rational faculty for itself to lie in. In the coda, the poet queries the desirability (or imperative?) of a withdrawal. The possibility of a destination is set against the potentiality of human aspiration. The concluding question exploits the imagery of a past era of sail ("fathoms, tacking") to cast doubt on the very notion of direction. The poem constitutes a further reworking of issues which Thomas's meditative lyrics work at and work over again and again. As the first line has it, "It was never easy".

In "History" (44) the same preoccupation is given a collage narrative rather than a dialogically philosophical form. The focus is rigidly Western – as if to concentrate (in Yeatsian fashion) on familiar descriptions of the modern engine of "Historia", as typifying the "glory" and "riddle" of "mankind" – and possibly the "jest".[25] In neo-Platonic style, the poem develops a comparative contrast between darkness and light – which is here complicated by playing historical stages off against an eschatological schedule modelled on diurnal development – morning to sundown. So there is a progression from the "Greek radiance", through the "midday" of Christ's crucifixion, on into the impact of Reformation on Mediaevalism, discovery of the New World and into the eventide of institutionalised science, with lights burning in a "million laboratories". The eras are deftly evoked, perhaps too deftly and it is not quite evident how far this might be a parody of conventionalised "History". Such an aspect of interpretation might depend on how the reader responds to the suggestive vignette: for example, "... A vessel took off / into navigable waters to discover how mutinous / was the truth". The predicated mutiny seems to depend on the relation between heart and intellect. The priests of the "Machine" are left to their attempt to turn barbarism into insight; the poem does not venture to indicate how this endeavour might result or whether the glory that was Greece is tongue-in-the-cheek "quotationality" or the soldier's conversion a recycled piety. The answer may not be "far off" – but the question remains.

In "Message" (56) Thomas declares that the mystery is "irrelevant". Birdsong is represented as the language of God, "offering friendship" (a perception musically perfected in the work of Olivier Messiaen). The epiphany of today is enough – and will be remembered as "wonderful". Attentive, still arguing with himself, the poet likens the chirping to an "injection" and suggests that it can cancel pain or worry, "before and after".

The technological realm is further introduced into this auditory Arcadia in terms of X-rays which (subverting the Western "ocularcentrism"[26] of the perspectival – and masculinist? – gaze) affirm the benignity of "love's growth" within our living organism. Borrowing, as often, from Eliot's word hoard, Thomas proposes that humankind has been, historically, anaesthetized on "a table", but the scalpel's steel has been "plied" by no surgeon but by "life" itself, characterised as "green". The poem looks forward to the patient's awakening from the experience, the resurgence of "tomorrow". Like the bird (like Sam in *Casablanca* and Hill's Offademand), the poet will "sing it for you / all over gain".

In the penultimate poem in the volume, "Revision" (69), the poet offers apology to the writers of hymns, "if levity deputises / for an Amen". In fact, Thomas's "Amen" employs both levity and ontological solemnity in seeking to offer benediction to the peculiar world of the twentieth century *fin de siècle*. In doing so, he concentrates on the short, self-querying poem ("lyric" seems a misnomer for Thomas's sceptically meditative style): added together, such poems constitute a collage of probes into the meaning of postmodern existence which cast interrogative light on each other. The major motifs concern physical suffering, spiritual belief (and doubt) and the omnipresence of scientific technology as environment for contemporary being. If Wales is the local particularity which illuminates a global harshness of bodily reality, then "Abercuawg" or "Love" constitute an "outre monde" – here a spiritual alternative rather than a revolutionary projection.[27] Such a "world" throws the physical reality itself into relief and calls for a change of consciousness. For the poet's "Amen" is less an expression of final assent than a challenge directed at the transfiguration of science into a holistic self-accountability, within the planetary environment and under the sign of *agape*. There are many signs in contemporary science itself that Thomas's message has not constituted bardic anachronism but intellectual prophecy.

Thomas has succeeded in forming an individual style out of the language games of postmodernity, without it quite qualifying for the dubious honorific of being labelled "postmodernist". I imagine he would prefer it this way, although his earlier claims of minor relevance[28] were unduly modest. The major influences on his later work appear to be the poems of Yeats and Eliot – a duumvirate suggestive of prime relevance and affectivity for the poet strong[29] enough to be able to appropriate their rich contributions. On the whole, Thomas has succeeded in this – avoiding the worst theatricalities of Yeats's grand manner and transcending the tortuous self-abasement of Eliot's later mannerisms. He has incorporated themes and modes of textual procedure which ground his writing in modernist precedent and yet project his vision through the postmodern towards the next millennium. The effect is unique:

> ... Before what cradle
> do the travellers from afar,
> strontium and plutonium, hold out
>   their thin gifts?
>
> (*Experimenting*, 65)

The Magi[30] of both Yeats and Eliot lie behind these lines – as does their idea that the Epiphany, as a story, is supremely relevant to an era of flux – far more so than any rationalist metanarrative. Yet the radically interrogative mode is Thomas's own, as are the halting rhythm and spare, updated diction. And considered in itself – as if a quotation from some canny Greek papyrus or a terse message from some outer space power – the lines encapsulate the poet's contemporary contribution: radical questioning of the meaning of being and becoming, evocation of the scientific–technological forces that have been unleashed into the present world, embodiment of the essentially human transaction of gift exchange in the face of wonder. Thomas's "Amen" incorporates just such phenomena: and it remains a sphere of original interrogation – as well as a Welsh priest's intertextual version of "Shantih shantih shantih".

Notes

1. R. S. Thomas, *Experimenting with an Amen* (Macmillan/Papermac, 1988).
2. See Chapter 4 above.
3. See Joel Kovel, *The Radical Spirit: Essays on Psychoanalysis and Society* (Free Association Books, 1988).
4. For an account of Thomas's earlier work see Dennis Brown, "Vernon Watkins and R. S. Thomas", *British Poetry*, vol. 2: *1950–1990*, ed. Brian Docherty (Macmillan, forthcoming). See also D. Z. Phillips, *R. S. Thomas: Poet of the Hidden God – Meaning and Mediation in the Poetry of R. S. Thomas* (Macmillan, 1986) and J. P. Ward, *The Poetry of R. S. Thomas* (Poetry Wales Press, 1987). For even later poems see R. S. Thomas, *The Echoes Return Slow* (Macmillan, 1988).
5. For the sentiments and language in this sentence see Donella H. Meadows, Dennis L. Meadows and Jørgen Randers, *Beyond*

Confronting Global Collapse – The Envisioning a Sustainable Future-Limits (Chelsea Green, 1992).

6. William Shakespeare, *The Complete Works*, ed. Stanley Wells and Gary Taylor, from *Richard II*, Act 2, Scene 1 (Clarendon Press, 1988), p. 375.

7. Quoted in D. Z. Phillips, *R. S. Thomas: Poet of the Hidden God*, p. 69.

8. See my chapter "Vernon Watkins and R. S. Thomas" in *British Poetry*, vol. 2. For poems in *H'm* and other collections see R. S. Thomas, *Later Poems 1972–1982* (Macmillan, 1984).

9. George Macbeth, "Owl", in (most popularly) *The New Poetry*, an anthology selected and introduced by A. Alvarez (Penguin, 1967), pp. 211–12.

10. Pierre Teilhard de Chardin, *The Phenomenon of Man*, with an introduction by Sir Julian Huxley, translator not acknowledged (Collins: Fontana Books, 1969).

11. See, for instance, "A Peasant", R. S. Thomas, *Selected Poems 1946–1968* (Bloodaxe Books, 1986), p. 11.

12. "Song at the Year's Turning", *ibid.*, p. 36.

13. I mean this in the sense of Marshall McLuhan's *The Gutenberg Galaxy*. I hope to elaborate in a future book what I take to be the complicity of traditional academic philosophy with printed "Grammatology" – and the distortions of truth effected thereby.

14. *The Modern Theologians: An Introduction to Christian Theology in the Twentieth Century*, vol. II, ed. David F. Ford (Blackwell, 1989), p. 293.

15. Jürgen Moltmann, *Theology Today: Two Contributions Towards Making Theology Present*, trans. John Bowden (SCM, 1988), p. 94.

16. See Phillips, *R. S. Thomas: Poet of the Hidden God, passim.*

17. *Ibid.*, pp. 92–3.

18. T. H. Huxley, "On the Physical Basis of Life", printed in his collected works of 1892, reprinted in *Victorian Prose and Poetry*, The Oxford Anthology of English Literature, ed. Lionel Trilling and Harold Bloom (Oxford University Press, 1973), p. 287.

19. See Docherty (ed.), *British Poetry*, vol. 2: *1950–1990*.

20. Cf. Frank Kermode, *The Sense of an Ending: Studies in the Theory of Fiction* (Oxford University Press, 1966).

21. Wordsworth on Isaac Newton, *The Prelude*, III, p. 63; *Wordsworth: Poetical Works*, p. 509.

22. *Chambers English Dictionary* (Cambridge, 1989), p. 63.

23. The title of a Yeats poem of 1933. See W. B. Yeats, *The Collected Poems* (Macmillan, 1967), p. 265.

24. "Had we come all that way"; cf. "Journey of the Magi", "were we led all that way", T. S. Eliot, *Complete Poems and Plays*, p. 104; "... where you began", cf. "arrive where we started", "Little Gidding", *ibid.*, p. 197.

25. Cf. Pope on "Man": "Great Lord of all things, yet a prey to all; / Sole judge of truth, in endless error hurled: / The glory, jest, and riddle of the world!" (Alexander Pope, *An Essay on Man II*, pp. 16–18, here quoted from *The Norton Anthology of English Literature*, vol. I, ed. M. H. Abrams and others (W. W. Norton, 1968), p. 1727).

26. See, for instance, Steve Connor in "Deconstruction and John Ashbery's 'Sortes Vergilianae'", in *Contemporary Poetry Meets Modern Theory*, ed. Antony Easthope and John O. Thompson (Harvester/Wheatsheaf, 1991), p. 14 and footnote 10, p. 18.
27. Cf. Christian Miquel's formulation in Chapter 7 above.
28. "I play on a small pipe, a little aside from the main road. But thank you for listening." Thomas on his work, quoted by D. Z. Phillips, *The Poet of the Hidden God*, p. 20.
29. In Harold Bloom's sense. See *The Anxiety of Influence: a Theory of Poetry* (Oxford University Press, 1973), *passim*.
30. Cf. "The Magi", W. B. Yeats, *Collected Poems*, p. 141; "Journey of the Magi", T. S. Eliot, *Complete Poems and Plays*, pp. 103–4.

10
Conclusion

R. S. Thomas's *Experimenting with an Amen* carries the argument of this book virtually into the nineties – especially if a realistic reader-reception period is allowed.[1] However, all but one of the poets considered above belong/ed to a now ageing generation. It was that generation, I have implied throughout, which negotiated the emergence of postmodernity and evaluated its implication in the remnants of both modernity and modernism. Yet we are clearly now in a newer situation – if only because of the widespread assimilation of the postmodern thesis itself – and there are many fresh voices which have sought to define our current situation. Whilst working on this book I have read, for instance, *The New British Poetry: 1968–88*[2] and *Contemporary Poetry Meets Modern Theory*,[3] both of which are mainly concerned with the work of younger poets. I should have liked myself to have considered the contributions of Roy Fisher, Lee Harwood and Tom Raworth, in particular, not to mention some more recent American poets. However, I am not sure my sense of the "Poetry of Postmodernity" would have been much modified, though it would have been enriched. But any book has to end somewhere. Since the Second World War there has been a dialogical relationship between English and American poets (most dramatically symbolised in the now almost mythical marriage of Sylvia Plath and Ted Hughes) which has created a privileged, even rarified, space for the representation of quasi-global postmodernity. That has been the focus of the book.

In more general terms and especially in the more recent era of course, such an Anglo/American "special relationship" begins to fall apart. Put another way, the very perception of a "global village" or "One World" condition has inevitably encouraged the multifarious "Englishes" of the planet to reject past marginalisation and speak fully from their own situations – whether in "postmodernised" terms or not. On the one hand, poetry in English must now more than ever include significant contributions from a near-galaxy of postcolonial countries, on the other, there have been eloquent representations in

134

all larger English-speaking countries from disparate regional, ethnic or gender groups which would have little desire to be decoded in relation to a notional Anglo/American aesthetic field. Whereas in the aftermath of World War Two Anglo/American poetics might seem to have been at the forefront of global moral and intellectual consciousness, even thirty years later this was already increasingly outdated – both abroad and "at home". The "Canon" (largely a construct of Marxists and feminists?) has been for some time under attack, while "minority" poets have slowly become heard. This has resulted in a literary flourishing far wider and, more interesting, than any single book could begin to acknowledge or assess. It has, indeed, been the case that "The Empire Writes Back"[4] – but so too have numerous other identity groups unentranced by the traditional categorisations of literary modernity and who, for whatever reason, have inherited English as a medium of expressivity.

At the same time, the implication of mainstream poetry in the largely passé conventions produced by the print revolution has begun to make much of it begin to appear anachronistic. There has been something of a revival of oral verse and poetic performance art and, at the same time, the possibilities of "concrete poetry" and hypertext art have been tried out. Most particularly, as noted in my Introduction, the supervention of electronic balladeering, as developed by the more imaginative performers, has begun to take over the very prophetic ground I have claimed for the poets considered above. I hold to the discriminations and descriptions I have made. But in broader terms, it would be a strangely recalcitrant critic who would maintain that Larkin's "Annus Mirabilis" was more relevant than Bob Dylan's "The Times They Are a-Changin'" or Tony Harrison's "A Kumquat for John Keats" than Dire Straits' "Brothers in Arms". Both Larkin and Harrison have been adroit and powerful practitioners of "Gutenberg" verse; the point here is not to question their talent but to mark a cultural shift brought about by the possibilities of postmodern media – a shift itself acknowledged in Harrison's television version of "V". Just as it is not now poets but courageous TV and newspaper reporters who are the "unacknowledged legislators of the world", so it is to the popular lyric performer that we commonly look to articulate "thoughts that do often lie too deep for tears" ("Yesterday", "Someone saved my life tonight", "Would you know my name ....?").

I believe, then, that while the "Poetry of Postmodernity" has done an important job in mediating (at a highly intelligent level) between the eras of modernity and postmodernity and between the aesthetics of modernism and postmodernism, it has also marked a point of transition in the role that printed poetry can now play within the later postmodern era. The new media render National Curriculum distinctions between metaphor and simile, alliteration and onomatopoeia, as irrelevant as Mediaeval subdivisions between the powers of minor angels. They communicate through a materially ideal realm of panaesthetic images and sounds unfixable in any known rhetorical formulations. Traditionally, English poetry had precisely specialised in both images and sound effects. In the early twentieth century Ezra Pound (doyen of modernist poetics) had restressed their importance ("phanopoeia" and "melopoeia").[5] Wyndham Lewis satirised his emphasis through the figure of Horace Zagreus[6] in *The Apes of God*:

> I impart a musical art. The last thing you must look for is the message of an orderly sentence – the significance lies in the impact of the image … it gets you in the guts like a bomb or it doesn't.[7]

Pound's stance and programme now seem like the last-ditch stand of a "poets' poet", already acutely aware of the persuasive power of new media and forms of message. It is fitting that one of the last vignettes we have of him is that given by Allen Ginsberg, who brought the songs of both Dylan and The Beatles to the ancient sage at Rapallo.[8]

However, Pound and Ginsberg were alike in prioritising creative imagination – in whatever medium: the art itself came first. Yet, at the current moment, many university departments which have traditionally fostered and expounded the principles of such art are in danger of being swamped under a deluge of cultural "theory": it is certainly theory rather than, for instance, contemporary poetic texts which dominate the lists of academic publishing houses. This is peculiarly ironic, since theory is inherently a Gutenberg phenomenon – even when its concern is with the new media. Despite its insights into the "death of the author", intertextuality or reader reception, its arguments are relentlessly structured in print terms: the frozen immobility of elaborately defined concepts; the extrapolation of such terms through cumulative linear rhetoric; the polysyllabic consecration of the whole text to sentence-by-sentence, paragraph-after-paragraph, Gutenberg grammatology. It is baffling that cultural studies should be so mesmerised by this kind of second-rate philosophising unless the phenomenon itself is seen as a traumatised reaction to the shock of the media explosion – what McLuhan would have called a "rear-view mirror" attempt to frame the new realities in terms of the very conventions they challenge. Literary studies, in particular, should be centred on revelatory texts not befuddled by a new scholasticism concerning the meaning of meaning. For it is such texts which can alert us to the nature of our contemporary situation. As for theory, our philosophers will do that for us – and better.

Of course, it is not only literary texts that are revelatory: there are relevant paintings, songs, videos, etc. – and sometimes, yes, the words of the prophet are written on the subway walls. However, my argument above has been that certain Anglo/American poets since the Second World War have, in fact, provided important scans of the postmodern terrain. And perhaps the first thing to notice in what they have registered is simply the perceived insubstantiality of the contemporary – their heightened awareness that "all that is solid melts into air".[9] This perception has been abroad since, at the least, Marx's prophetic words in the nineteenth century, but when town planners view such projects as the Canary Wharf development in terms of some ten to twenty years' use (and even that scenario has been superseded by events), we are into an even faster, "turn-around" world. Poetry has been quick to register this. Auden's version of Ariel as the instant constructor of chimerical scenarios was merely an early allegory of what has become material fact – the fluxive rise and fall, visions and revisions, construction and deconstruction of buildings, systems, boundaries and theories in perpetual motion. The phenomenon is attested to in Ginsberg's "Vortex", Hill's "Mercia" and Ashbery's "Wave". For better or worse, the spirit of Heraclitus presides over the spectacle of the postmodern. All change, is the constant formula. As R. S. Thomas has phrased it with typical bleakness, "The soiled fountain / plays, where the scientists gather / bacteria" ("Cures", *Experimenting*, 66).

Another important feature of the "Poetry of Postmodernity", as of recent fiction, has been a (paradoxical?) sense of the "Presence of the Past". It is probably the very awareness of the insubstantiality of current social constructions which has led to the variable dialogue between contemporaneity and history in such poetry as "The Sea and the Mirror", *Dream Songs*, "Mercian Hymns" or *Experimenting with an Amen*. In this regard, there has been the powerful precedent of *The Waste Land* – for whatever Eliot's magisterial criticism might have suggested, the 1922 poem does not constitute a safe stronghold in the "universal" values of the past but a radical questioning of both past and present significations *sub specie aeternitatis*.[10] In postmodern poetry such questioning is carried on less by collagistic "quotationality" than as a continuous recycling of past events and tropes in dialogical relationship to readings of the present scenario. This seems peculiarly in tune with the rise of nationalist myths since the Cold War began to unravel[11] – and becomes dourly confirmed in current East European tensions, where virtually tribal memories impact against the hectic demands of a triumphalist global capitalism – often on lands once flattened by "the roller / Of wars, wars, wars". Thomas's late invocation of Yeats's "gyres" represents, as it were, a double recycling – querying the meaning of historical event by redeploying a key figure in the precedent master's construction of historical process. Even Ashbery's Whitmanesque "Wave" bears a full freight of the detritus of the past – as Hill's "Mercia" is bogged down in it. Postmodernity remains haunted by memories: it seems unlikely that future poetry can suspend this temporal dialogue without becoming merely bland.

At the same time, just as "high" poetry since 1945 has been increasingly dominated by environmental issues so any significant new poetry must construe "Waste Land" as much a material possibility as a spiritual warning. The poetry of Ted Hughes has been especially admonitory in this regard – "Crow"'s eye-view sees the planet largely as a feeding-field and one which becomes less and less promising when the poem "alights". In "The Sea and the Mirror" the ageing Prospero was still able to see the resources of the "island" as guaranteed – now to be yielded up to a postcolonial Caliban. But in Ashbery's work, most particularly, natural wealth is given over to the machinations of "men who sit down to their vast desks on Monday to begin planning the week's notations" ("Decoy", 105). And if Ashbery's scene is largely a metropolitan one, Thomas's scenario has become global – from the exploited land of rural Wales to that of the entire, satellite-orbited earth. Such poets offer as sobering a vision of the depletion and poisoning of Creation's wealth as that of certain more recent environmental scientists. And there is a quite direct descriptive line from Ginsberg's scan of industrial America to, say, Derek Jarman's acutely observed "Modern Nature" at Dungeness.[12] At the starkest point is Plath's final moon-view of a suicided planet: "She is used to this sort of thing". It has been a major function of written poetry, since at least the time of Shakespeare, to remind an increasingly scientific culture of the richness of the natural realm – and our responsive place in it. The "Poetry of Postmodernity" has intensified the urgency of this message throughout a period of quite wholesale technological ravagement of the world.

In such a situation it should come as no surprise that this poetry has not so much colluded with the scientistic "Death of God" literature pioneered by such as Conrad and Hardy as sought to negotiate with the emergence of a spiritual "return of the repressed".[13] From late Auden through to late Thomas this has even effected alliances with forms of specifically Christian tradition – whether liturgical catholicism or *via negativa* mysticism – a phenomenon which throws its own ironic light on the scientistic puberty rites of the Victorian era, when losing one's faith was as fashionable as losing one's virginity in the 1960s. However, it was the far from orthodox Sylvia Plath who posed an unanswerable question to her fifties' American education: "Once one has seen God, what is the remedy?" The extraordinary Berryman added postmodern angst to Donne's spiritual wrestling when he wrote: "Dinch me, dark God". And the ace poetic surfer of New York postmodernity, John Ashbery, has floated out of his highly self-conscious puzzlement the suggestion that "we must ... put our faith in some superior power which will carry us beyond into a region of light and timelessness" ("The System", 136). It is not that such recent poetry offers firm convictions concerning a neglected teleology, let alone that it tells us how to live; but certainly it has opened again issues which might have seemed closed forever at the dawn of this century. These, I believe, should remain pressing for poets as we look forward to the next century, in increasingly complex times.

Richard Rorty's title *Contingency, Irony and Solidarity*[14] might stand as the concerned thinker's slogan throughout the nineties. All the poets whose aesthetic "zones" have been the matter of this book have manifest connections to each of the three terms. Yet, in what particular way have they expanded Rorty's idea of "poeticity"? I think radical "poeticism" has the particular advantage over prose fiction that *rhythmical* rhetoric is at the centre of its project. The distinction is less one of imaginative power than of expressive medium: textual poetry uniquely combines oral and print conventions through the maximum conjunction of physical, psychic and intellectual faculties. Its disadvantage is that not many people today have the perceptive openness, focused attention span or respect for poetic insight which would make it seem worthy of careful appraisal. The problem deserves the careful attention of all in education, at any level. For poetry speaks a holistic form of truthfulness. And the "Poetry of Postmodernity" has succeeded in bending commercial tropes and idioms back upon themselves to express the "condition" we are living in and intimate that there are more things in heaven and earth than are dreamt of in our technocracy. That is worthy of everyone's attention.

Books have particular limitations in the "electric age". If you want to find out the current state-of-play in genetic engineering, geo-politics, environmental understanding or AIDS research, books usually come too late; conferences or even a good television pro-gramme are more able to provide relevant , up-to-date knowledge. Printed poetry, also, suffers from time-lag, but as Pound wrote, "POETRY IS NEWS THAT STAYS NEWS". *An Essay on Man, The Prelude, In Memoriam* or *Four Quartets* still encapsulate an age, for all time, better than any other writing. This holds true for the "Poetry of Postmodernity". Here contingency, irony and solidarity come encoded as the nearest our culture gets towards wisdom, and the greatest of these is solidarity – since without it we are doomed. For poets of the future, I offer Geoffrey Hill's words on Péguy – but with reference to the poets discussed above:

Take that for your example.

Notes

1. It is an increasingly depressing situation that between conception, composition, acceptance-negotiation, publication, distribution and eventual reader reception, the printed word always comes late in a world of instantaneous information. One can only hope that cogency can make up for the time-lag.
2. *The New British Poetry: 1968–88*, ed. Gillian Allnutt, Fred D'Aguiar, Ken Edwards and Eric Mottram (Paladin/Grafton Books, 1988). See also John Mole, *Passing Judgements: Poetry in the Eighties* (Bristol Classical Press, 1989).
3. *Contemporary Poetry Meets Modern Theory*, ed. Antony Easthope and John O. Thompson (Harvester/Wheatsheaf, 1991). Peter Brooker's

interesting piece on Tom Raworth (pp. 153–65) reminds us of the "Black Mountain" poets whose work I have neglected here, although I nearly included a chapter on Robert Duncan whose poetry I have particularly admired.

4. See Index and above.
5. See *Literary Essays of Ezra Pound*, ed. with an Introduction by T. S. Eliot (Faber and Faber, 1968), pp. 26–7.
6. For this identification see my *Intertextual Dynamics*, p. 147.
7. Wyndham Lewis, *The Apes of God* (Penguin, 1965), p. 402.
8. As recounted in Humphrey Carpenter, *A Serious Character: The Life of Ezra Pound* (Faber and Faber, 1988), p. 897.
9. Marx's celebrated phrase. See Marshall Berman, *All that is Solid Melts into Air: The Experience of Modernity* (Verso, 1983).
10. For a study of the neo-Platonic aspects of this see my "Plato and the Earlier Eliot", in *Platonism and the English Literary Imagination*, ed. Anna Baldwin and Sarah Hutton (Cambridge University Press, forthcoming).
11. For an acute early account of this see Neal Ascherson, "Eastern Europe on the Move" in *New Times: The Changing Face of Politics in the 1990s*, ed. Stuart Hall and Martin Jacques (Lawrence and Wishart in association with *Marxism Today*, 1989), pp. 22–9.
12. Derek Jarman, *Modern Nature: The Journals of Derek Jarman* (Vintage, 1992).
13. I have written at length about this phenomenon in *Modern Literature in English and the Christian Theme: The Death of God and the New Life*, which has yet to find a publisher.
14. See Index and above.

Index

142